Information 2.0

New models of information production,
distribution and consumption

Information 2.0

New models of information production, distribution and consumption

Martin De Saulles

 facet publishing

© Martin De Saulles 2012

Published by Facet Publishing
7 Ridgmount Street, London WC1E 7AE
www.facetpublishing.co.uk

Facet Publishing is wholly owned by CILIP: the Chartered Institute of Library and Information Professionals.

British Library Cataloguing in Publication Data
A catalogue record for this book is available from the British Library.

ISBN 978-1-85604-754-8

First published 2012

Text printed on FSC accredited material.

Mixed Sources
Product group from well-managed
forests and other controlled sources
www.fsc.org Cert no. SA-COC-1565
© 1996 Forest Stewardship Council
FSC

Typeset from author's files in 10/13 pt Palatino Linotype and Frutiger by Flagholme Publishing Services
Printed and made in Great Britain by MPG Books Group, UK.

Dedication

For Jerome, my wonderful son

Contents

Preface ix

1   Introduction 1
What is information? 2
The foundations of the information society 3
The internet as a driver of change 4
The big challenges of big data 6
What about the information providers? 8
New ways of creating information 10
Where do we put all this information? 10
Why information matters 11

2   New models of information production **13**
Introduction 13
Blogs and the challenge to publishers 14
Wikis and collaborative publishing 22
Search engines and what they know 25
Podcasting and the democratization of the media 29
The challenge of big data 32
Concluding comments 35
Questions to think about 35

3   New models of information storage **37**
Introduction 37
Preserving the internet 38
How organizations store information 41
Legal requirements 44
Data mining 46

Collection digitization 48
Keeping it all safe 51
Storage at the personal level 51
Putting it in the cloud...53
Our digital footprints..54
The future of storage...56
Concluding comments 58
Questions to think about..58

4   **New models of information distribution**............................**59**
Introduction..59
The architecture of the internet 60
Distribution and disintermediation 63
The new intermediaries 66
Online video – we're all celebrities now................................69
Open government and the internet 73
Threats to the open web 80
Concluding comments 82
Questions to think about..83

5   **New models of information consumption**...........................**85**
Introduction..85
Information consumption devices..86
Looking beyond the artefact...90
Information ecosystems: gilded cages or innovation hotbeds? ...94
Returning to an open web 98
Rent or buy? 101
Making sense of it all..103
Implications for information professionals 107
Concluding comments 109
Questions to think about...109

6   **Conclusion** **111**
Introduction...111
Implications for information professionals 111
Implications for publishers 116
Implications for society 120
Concluding comments 122

References **125**

Index **135**

Preface

There is a certain ironyin the fact that I have attempted to summarize some of the key challenges facing the information sector through the medium of the book. Perhaps a series of posts on my blog (www.mdesaulles.net) or uploaded videos of some of the talks and lectures I have given during the preparation of this book would have been more appropriate for the digital age we find ourselves moving into. With bookshops and libraries closing all around us, does the book have a future as a means for distributing information? Only time will tell what the future holds for the paper book but I would wager that the monograph, in a variety of published outputs, will continue to be a key format for the transfer of ideas and arguments. What is definitely changing is the economics of publishing, with new technologies such as e-books and new forms of self-publishing challenging the established practices of an industry that has been built around the production and sale of physical items. Digital formats, as this book shows, allow information to flow more freely in ways that bypass many of the traditional bottlenecks and gatekeepers such as printers, bookshops and libraries. For end-users this can mean an increase in choice of where and how they consume information while for new entrants such as Google and Amazon there are novel ways to capture value from these new information flows.

My intention in writing this book is to provide an overview of the digital information landscape and explain the implications of the technological changes for the information industry, from publishers and broadcasters to the information professionals who manage information in all its forms. It is not possible in a book of this length to detail every aspect of these changes and challenges but I have attempted to summarize their broader implications through the use of real examples and case studies. By providing examples of organizations and individuals that are seizing on the opportunities thrown up by this once-in-a-generation technological shift I hope the reader is able to better understand where we may be going both as information consumers but also in terms of broader societal changes.

The structure of the book is fairly linear in that each chapter explores aspects of the information life-cycle, including production, distribution, storage and consumption. However, I hope I have been able to show how these stages are closely intertwined within the broader global information ecosystem that is emerging based on the digitization of content in all its forms. One of the key themes that emerges from this book is the way that organizations, public and commercial, are blurring their traditional lines of responsibility. Amazon is moving from simply selling books to offering the hardware and software for reading them. Apple still makes computer hardware but also manages the world's leading marketplaces for music and software applications. Google maintains its position as the most popular internet search engine but has also digitized millions of copies of books from the world's leading academic libraries. At the heart of these changes are the emergence of cheap computing devices for decoding and presenting digital information and a network which allows the bits and bytes to flow freely, for the moment at least, from producer to consumer.

I hope that this book will be of interest to students on information management and publishing courses as well as practitioners who wish to better understand the dynamics that are shaping the industry they work in. Each chapter contains short case studies which have been chosen to illustrate particular issues and challenges facing the information industry. At the end of each chapter are questions for further discussion. These are deliberately provocative and are intended to stimulate discussion and debate.

While the digital revolution is impacting on everyone who works with information, sometimes negatively, my objective has been to show that the opportunities outweigh the risks for those who take the time to understand what is going on. Information has never been more abundant and accessible so those who know how to manage it for the benefit of others in the digital age will be in great demand. I hope that this book will help you on that journey.

Martin De Saulles

CHAPTER 1

Introduction

In 2011, according to Gantz and Reinsel (2011), the amount of information created and replicated globally was 1.8 zettabytes; that is, 1.8 trillion gigabytes or, if stored on DVDs, enough for that pile of discs to reach the moon, come back to earth and back to the moon again. By 2020, technology consultancy IDC estimates this will have grown to 35 zettabytes and will present huge challenges for those tasked with managing this information. For the last 50 years we have been told that developed economies are moving beyond their industrial foundations and into a post-industrial, information age. These claims by writers and researchers such as Machlup (1962), Toffler (1970), Bell (1973) and Stonier (1983) were based on the observations that work was becoming more information-focused and economies were more reliant on services than industrial outputs. Analysis of the economic statistics since the early 1960s supports these observations with the service sector accounting for approximately three-quarters of the economic output of the USA and Europe. Accompanying these developments has been the explosion in digital technologies that have transformed the ways we create, distribute and consume information and, it would be fair to say, have realized the claims that we are moving to an information society.

This book builds on the work of previous writers and considers the implications of some of the most significant changes of the previous 20 years for information professionals and the rapidly changing environment they find themselves in. Just as the invention of the movable type printing press in the 15th century helped transform society through making information more accessible to the masses, so new methods of publishing based around digital tools are shaping our society in the 21st century. For those unwilling to change the way they work these changes present a threat, but for those, information professionals included, who understand the potential of these new digital publishing platforms and the forces that drive them there are enormous benefits. The following chapters will take you through some of the key technologies behind this revolution and explain how they developed, who is using them and what it means for both information professionals and society at large. At the end of each chapter are questions to prompt further discussion and readers are encouraged to spend a few minutes working through them before moving on to the next chapter. The remainder of this chapter will set the scene for the issues addressed in this book and provide a broader context within which to think about the digital revolution we find ourselves in.

What is information?

While this may seem like a strange question, particularly in a book aimed primarily at those who work with information, it is worth considering, even if only to set the parameters for what is to be considered in future chapters. In one sense, information is everywhere in that we ascribe meanings to the objects and forms around us. Dark clouds could be said to impart information as they warn us of impending rain and similarly the road sign outside a school tells us to slow down as there may be children crossing. The shape and health of our bodies are defined by the information contained in the genetic instructions within our DNA. However, for the purposes of this book we are concerned with the information that is created by humans for education, entertainment and commerce. Before looking in more detail at some of the technologies that are shaping the production of such information it would be useful to clarify some of the terms that are often used, sometimes confusingly, to describe information: data, information, knowledge. Although there is some debate about the meaning of these terms and the boundaries between them, they provide a useful way of thinking about information and its value. The notion of a knowledge value chain whereby raw data is turned into usable information and, through human application, becomes knowledge emerged in the early 1970s and was the foundation of knowledge management as an area of organizational activity. Henry (1974) developed this idea and was one of the first to make a differentiation between the stages that go into the creation of knowledge. In his model, data is the raw, unstructured output of various activities that, on its own, has little or no meaning. In a retail setting it might be the data that is produced by supermarket checkouts that lists product codes and prices. This data can be turned into usable information when it is placed into a broader context of the items that the codes refer to, how many items were sold at particular prices and over a specific time period. This is information that store managers can use to work out what products are selling well and the impact that different pricing strategies are having. In Henry's model, knowledge is created when those managers use the information to make decisions about which products to order more of, what price to sell them at and which products to drop. Knowledge is the application of understanding and previous experience to the information that is presented. We will return to the notion of knowledge management in the final chapter but at this stage it is important to explain how the term 'information' is used throughout this book. In essence it primarily refers to this middle stage in knowledge creation but in the context of some of the technologies under discussion it could also be said to refer to data in its rawest state. This is particularly true in Chapter 4 where we look at information distribution and the networks that carry the bits and bytes of the information revolution. The data that flows over these pipes and airwaves is binary and, until it is decoded by the devices at the user's end, would make no sense to anyone. With this clarification in mind, let's now consider some of the most significant innovations of the previous 50 years, which have resulted in the upheavals to the information industries and society more generally.

The foundations of the information society

It is really the combination of computing technologies with communication networks that has formed the basis for the digital revolution we are now living in. Chapter 4 explains in some detail how the internet has evolved from its academic and military origins in the 1970s to its present state as a global information network. However, it is worth remembering that the internet was not originally designed as a mass communications system on which billions of individuals and millions of organizations would come to depend. Early proponents of the notion that western economies were morphing into information societies envisaged far more centralized information networks controlled by a combination of the state and private enterprises rather than the almost anarchic network that is the internet. As we will see in the final chapter, there are moves by a number of regulators, policy makers and corporate interests to reshape the internet into something more centrally controlled but, for the moment at least, we have a relatively open and accessible network. It is this openness, combined with the mass adoption of computing devices, deskbound and portable, that has encouraged the rampant innovation and development of information services since the 1990s. The traditional guardians of our telecommunication networks, companies such as BT, AT&T, Telstra, etc., were far more conservative in their approach to offering any information services beyond simple voice calls. While these companies are still important in maintaining the infrastructure of the internet, their significance as gatekeepers to electronic information resources is much diminished. The internet has shifted the balance of power to companies such as Google, Facebook and Amazon, which are the new information gatekeepers. In late 2011, Google and Amazon had a combined stock market value higher than that of AT&T, BT and Telstra. Alongside the rapid rise of information companies has been the growth of companies making the hardware through which we access their services. Personal computers are as much a part of office-based jobs as the desks they sit on, while netbooks, smartphones and tablets are also becoming essential items for the modern worker.

In some respects the changes wrought by these technological innovations have been, so far at least, less dramatic that futurologists such as Toffler (1970, 1980, 1990) predicted. His predictions that the education system will have disintegrated by the year 2000 and that offices would by now be paperless still seem some way off. However, the more general point that remote access to the world's information would be made possible by mass computing and communications networks has been realized. Never have so many people had access to so much information at their fingertips and the impact of this on societies around the world has hardly begun to be felt. As we shall see throughout this book, not only is access to information making the notion of an information society real, but the ability of individuals to create and share information is changing the structures of many industries, in particular the publishing sector.

The internet as a driver of change

Since 1995 we have gone from a world where there were approximately 10 million internet users to one where over 2 billion people are connected. Billions of e-mails are sent over this network every day and hundreds of millions of people search Google and other search engines for information spread across the plethora of web pages. According to the UK's Office for National Statistics (ONS), in 2011 three-quarters of UK households had a broadband internet connection, while over 90% of 16 to 24 year olds were users of social networking services such as Facebook and Twitter (ONS, 2011). The ways that internet services have impacted on how we find information, communicate, collaborate and purchase goods are rippling through society and forcing organizations and entire industries to restructure the ways they work. The music industry is an obvious example with the illegal sharing of MP3 files and the development of legal downloading services such as iTunes making older formats such as the CD and the business models surrounding them obsolete. The film industry is facing similar challenges as the internet presents users with a new channel for consuming media, and, via devices such as smartphones and tablets, the opportunity to break free from the television set in the living room. However, while some organizations may see the internet as a threat to their businesses, it has been argued by others that the broader economic benefits to society outweigh any possible disadvantages to particular interests. Consulting firm, McKinsey has estimated that the internet has accounted for more than one-fifth of GDP growth in mature economies from 2005 to 2010, is responsible for creating 2.6 new jobs for every one that is lost and that smaller companies which are heavy users of web technologies grow twice as fast as others (Manyika and Roxburgh, 2011). On a social level, it has been suggested that social media services such as Facebook and Twitter have been enablers for those involved in the Middle East uprisings in 2011, commonly referred to as the Arab Spring. The extent to which such services had a real influence is debatable, but the fact that the Egyptian Government shut down internet access for its citizens in early 2011 indicates the authorities feared how it was being used by those leading the protests (C. Williams, 2011).

Librarians and other information professionals were among the first to realize the importance of the internet to the provision of information services and the People's Network initiative launched in 2000 to connect every public library in the UK to the network is generally seen as having been a great success. However, in an age when most households have high-speed internet connections, is there a danger that this aspect of their service will become less relevant? This will be considered in later chapters when the issue of information literacy is examined. The flexibility of many information professionals to adapt to new technologies will be crucial here as the democratization of information access throws up new challenges and opportunities to help users navigate their way through the new digital landscape. While early public initiatives in many countries focused on encouraging companies and people to go online and sample the delights of the internet, there is a growing realization that simply providing someone with an internet connection and a computer does not automatically enhance their education. To update and paraphrase the well known commentator on information matters Barbara Quint, Google probably handles more reference enquiries in a day than have all the world's librarians over the last 100 years (Abram, 2007). In a world where most people's starting point for finding information is no longer the library but an internet search engine, the relevance of information professionals to modern life is under question. However, as we will see throughout this book, the opportunities for those who keep abreast of these changes are considerable. When everyone has access to the same information it will be those who can manipulate data for the competitive advantage of their users who will thrive.

It should be noted that challenges to libraries as well as the impact of libraries on the publishing industry is not a recent phenomenon. Shapiro and Varian (1999) note that the first circulating libraries in England sprung up in the 18th century when bookstores could not keep up with demand for popular novels and so started renting them out. At the time publishers were concerned that the commercial renting of books would undermine sales and reduce their profits. However, the greater availability of popular books encouraged more people to learn to read and ultimately increased the overall sale of books. As we will see in Chapter 4, similar concerns were and, to an extent, still are expressed by the larger music publishers who have blamed the rise of downloadable music for the decline of their profits. While there may be substance to these concerns, what is often missed, as with book publishers 250 years ago, is that business models change and technology combined with consumer preferences ultimately shape the way industries evolve. Shapiro and Varian point out that the number of frequent readers in England grew from 80,000 in 1800 to over 5 million by 1850. The decline of one industry is often accompanied by the rise of new ones:

> . . . it was the presence of the circulating libraries that killed the old publishing model, but at the same time it created a new business model of mass-market books. The for-profit circulating libraries continued to survive well into the 1950s. What killed them off was not a lack of interest in reading but rather the paperback book – an even cheaper way of providing literature to the masses.
>
> (Shapiro and Varian, 1999)

The rapid rise of e-books and e-book readers such as the Amazon Kindle is seen by many as a threat to traditional book shops and lending libraries, but, as we will see in later chapters, some of these institutions are adapting to this digital platform through extended and enhanced service offerings.

The big challenges of big data

Chapters 2 and 3 explore the new models of information production and the technologies that are being developed and deployed for the storage of the outputs of the data explosion of the 21st century. The exponential growth in data production has required the invention of new terms such as zettabyte and yottabyte to describe the quantities involved. A lot of this information is the result of the computerization of many business processes such as retail sales, product orders and stock control. Chapter 3 looks at the challenges that large retailers such as Walmart and Tesco face in trying to make sense of the data generated by the billions of products they sell to hundreds of millions of people each year. Analysts often refer to this as 'big data' as its storage, manipulation and analysis are pushing the boundaries of computing and information management capabilities. Similarly the move of many services to the internet are also throwing up new data challenges with web analytics becoming a new area for information professionals to move in to. Freely available and easy to use tools such as Google Analytics allow web managers, through the insertion of a few lines of code onto a website, to track how many people are visiting specific pages, how long they are staying, which sites referred them and what search terms they used to get there.

For content creators and publishers this offers immense opportunities to understand the behaviour of their consumers in ways that were never possible under traditional publishing platforms such as newspapers, magazines and books. Once a book or newspaper has been sold it is extremely difficult and often expensive for the publisher to know who has bought their content and what they are doing with it. The newsagent and bookshop have stood in between the publisher and reader, preventing any meaningful commercial relationship from developing. Newspaper subscriptions and publishers such as Reader's Digest which have engaged in direct sales are attempts to develop those relationships, but have always accounted for a minority of sales. By offering content via the web, publishers, particularly news producers, can bypass the newsagent and using web analytics software better understand how readers engage with their outputs. However, there is a potential danger that publishers may be too driven by the data and become less adventurous and creative in the content they commission. Knowing that readers are drawn to particular types of story may encourage more investment in those types of stories at the expense of less popular but possibly important writing.

McKinsey consultants, Manyika et al. (2011) argue that the challenges to organizations posed by managing big data are immense but also offer a way for companies and entire economies to profit from a new wave of innovation based around information management. They claim that while the amount of data generated globally is growing at an annual rate of 40% the growth in IT spending is only growing at an average of 5% per annum. A decrease in the costs of IT hardware will help address this imbalance but it also requires new ways of processing and understanding how this information can be used to increase efficiency. Manyika et al. claim that an extra 1.5 million data-savvy managers would be needed in the USA alone to take advantage of this information bonanza. In many ways this presents huge opportunities for information professionals if, as the authors believe, information is going to become the battle ground on which companies attain competitive advantage and economies move out of their moribund states triggered by the financial crises of 2008:

> Like other essential factors of production such as hard assets and human capital, it is increasingly the case that much of modern economic activity, innovation, and growth simply couldn't take place without data.
>
> (Manyika et al., 2011)

While many of the roles involved in making sense of big data will go to those with the mathematical and computing abilities not traditionally associated with library and information professionals, the core skills of organizing information at the heart of information management must surely play a part. Part of the responsibility for helping information professionals capitalize on these new roles will lie with the educational establishments that offer library and information courses. It is important that these courses reflect the changing nature of information work and, at the very least, help their students appreciate the implications of these changes to the jobs they will be applying for.

What about the information providers?

As we will see in Chapter 5, innovation and developments in the hardware that people use to access information resources have had a significant impact on the companies that offer information products and services. Alongside this, the rise of the internet as a distribution network for information services and the world wide web as a user-friendly interface to interrogate online databases have allowed new entrants into the marketplace that have been able to make use of a relatively open and widely used platform. This ease of access to information services for users has impacted on the role of many information professionals who have, for a number of years, been the experts on and gatekeepers to online information access. Anyone who has used online databases via providers such as Dialog will be aware that it is a very different experience from the simplicity of an internet search engine like Google. While Dialog and other information providers have migrated their services to the web, knowing how to select relevant databases and then search them efficiently still requires skill and at least a basic understanding of information retrieval techniques. For some types of search, information aggregators such as Dialog are still essential ports of call for information professionals. If you need access to patent filings, financial records of private companies or scientific research papers, then there are only a handful of paid information services that will suffice. However, other types of information, particularly news-related content, are becoming commoditized as many news publishers offer their stories for free via their websites. This has undermined the news aggregation services offered by DataStar, LexisNexis, Factiva and others, which have charged users, typically information professionals, to search and retrieve news stories from the world's newspapers. In 2002, Google launched its Google News service by aggregating 4000 news sources from around the world and providing free access via a search interface similar to the Google internet search page. Although initially focused on current affairs, in 2006 the company added an archive to the service offering users the ability to search through 200 years of news articles from a variety of sources.

The impact of Google News and other similar services on the traditional paid-for news aggregation services has been significant and companies like LexisNexis and Factiva are having to make a strong case to information professionals about why their fees are worth paying. One of their responses has been to offer services that are more closely integrated into the workflows of the organizations that require news information. The days of the information professional presenting a print-out of search results to an end-user and leaving them to decide what to do with it are coming to an end. Online information providers of all sorts are developing products that work within established business practices and technologies to create a smoother flow of information provision that attempts to deliver what is needed at the right time and place and in the most useful format. Paul Al-Nakaash, Head of Content Alliances at LexisNexis, recognizes these new pressures and the responses that are required if companies like his are to remain relevant:

> Aggregators must focus on meeting end user needs. It is no longer enough to have information if it is not available to a user at the appropriate time.
>
> (Al-Nakaash, 2011)

Factiva, part of the Dow Jones publishing group and a major provider of global information products and services, is also proactively developing new services to meet the challenges facing information aggregators. Its Factiva Publisher product allows organizations to integrate Factiva content with their own internal information, creating a closer integration between relevant internal and external content.

A more recent challenge to both traditional information publishers and aggregators comes from the rise of social media and user-generated content that bypasses the established publishing chain altogether. In Chapter 4, the commercial value of information generated by social media will be discussed with particular reference to the financial sector. While some might argue that social media services such as Facebook and Twitter are only concerned with trivial and insignificant issues, there is evidence, as we will see, that some of the posts and tweets when examined en masse contain nuggets of valuable insight.

New ways of creating information

While digital technologies and the internet have led to ever-increasing amounts of information being created and companies like Google have made it easier to search for what we want, the same technologies have also resulted in new models of information production. Cheaper and more powerful personal computers, audio and video production tools and the internet as a distribution network have allowed individuals and small companies to build information empires of their own. Podcasting is a good example of a service that brings together different technologies and standards, and which has been taken up by hundreds of thousands of micro-broadcasters, each catering for different audience niches, from beekeeping to yoga. Similarly blogging platforms such as WordPress and Blogger are being used by writers with specialist knowledge to share their expertise with a potential audience of over 2 billion internet users and, in some cases, earn a living from their endeavours. Linking podcasting and blogging is the RSS web format for pushing out information updates to subscribers, providing a broadcast-like experience to web users. The implications of these technologies for the publishing and broadcasting sectors are considered in Chapter 2 where examples of new companies which have based their successful and profitable businesses on blogging and podcasting are discussed. While large broadcasters and publishers are unlikely to be threatened by the rise of these new upstarts in the short term, it seems quite possible that over the longer term a network of multiple content producers will develop as it becomes cheaper and easier to build a media business. When you no longer need expensive printing presses or have to buy expensive broadcast licences from regulators and governments, then a more democratic and accessible media landscape may be the result. We are already seeing the signs of this through dramatic falls in newspaper sales and the amount of time many people in households with internet access spend watching mainstream television.

Where do we put all this information?

If, as discussed earlier in this chapter, consultants IDC and McKinsey are correct that the amount of data produced globally will continue to increase rapidly over the coming years, it will be an information management challenge to develop improved technologies for storing it. This will be particularly important where the information takes on an enhanced commercial value to organizations that use it for attaining a competitive advantage. One of the answers is the development of new compression techniques for reducing the amount of space required for storing digital data. Music fans have benefited from the compression of digital music files with the mass deployment of the MP3 and other audio compression techniques where source files can be reduced by up to 90% of their original size with little discernible loss of quality. Manyika et al. (2011) point out that in 2011 a $600 hard drive can be purchased that is capable of storing every digital music track ever recorded. Similar advances have been made with image and video compression that allow the easy storage and sharing of multimedia via smartphones, cameras and tablets. In Chapter 3 some of the ways that commercially valuable information is being stored are examined. These are presenting environmental as well as technological challenges to the hosting companies. Information-intensive companies such as Google and Facebook manage millions of computer servers which require large amounts of electricity both to power and cool them. In some cases, as we will see, the power requirements are being met by building data centres next to hydro-electric power stations with cooling issues being addressed by locating other centres in the Arctic Circle or under mountains.

Why information matters

This book is an attempt to give an overview of some of the most important developments taking place in the production, distribution, storage and consumption of information and what they mean for those who create information, the professionals who manage it and the people who consume it. The following chapters will expand upon the themes and issues touched on in this introduction and, through the use of examples, case studies and questions for further discussion, provide the reader with a better understanding of why digital information is transforming the ways we learn, work and play. Once information moves from the analogue realm into the digital sphere, radical and important changes take place. Computing devices are able to make sense of the 0s and 1s and allow the creation of new insights into what they mean and how they might be useful.

Google's book digitization project encapsulates what this transformation can mean for researchers and students around the world. Google estimated that in 2010 there were 130 million unique books across the world, many of them sitting on dusty library shelves inaccessible to those unable to physically visit that library (Jackson, 2010). Google's stated aim is to scan and create digital copies of all those books by 2020 with an estimated 15 million already scanned by the end of 2010. Although ongoing legal disputes call the viability of this project into question, it is still one of the most ambitious and important projects of its kind. By creating searchable copies of books that have been out of reach to most people and offering a freely accessible search interface to interrogate their contents, Google is opening up a large part of the world's information heritage to the masses.

While the Google Books project is only one example of the potential of digitized information for stimulating societal change and innovation, it illustrates what is possible when vision and technical capabilities are combined with hard cash. We are entering a perfect storm created by the convergence of low-cost and accessible tools that allow digital information to be accessed, manipulated and shared in ways never before possible. For content creators and information professionals there has never been a more exciting time to be alive.

CHAPTER 2
New models of information production

Introduction

That the amount of information being produced, stored, distributed and consumed is growing at a rapidly increasing rate is not in doubt. We saw evidence of this in the introductory chapter. The mass adoption of computing devices at home and at work and the rise of the internet as a distribution platform are the primary factors behind this growth. When information is digitized, the replication and sharing of it become easy and allow our transition from a pre-internet era of information scarcity to one of abundance. This chapter starts at the beginning of the information life cycle and looks at new models of information production based around new technologies such as blogs, podcasting and social media. The internet and mass computing are at the heart of these new models, some of which are evolutionary and others revolutionary. Their impact on the existing content creation industries will vary depending on the extent to which established organizations can adapt to new technologies. Podcasting and blogging, for example, are new activities but their outputs can be seen as evolutions of existing information formats. Podcasts can be seen as time-shifted radio while blogs, in some of their forms at least, are online journals or newspapers. Social networks such as Facebook and internet search engines such as Google, however, are producing new types of information that have no counterparts in the analogue world. The extent to which social networks can map the online communications between individuals and organizations allows companies such as Facebook and LinkedIn to understand our virtual relationships in unprecedented detail. Google's ownership of the search requests of its hundreds of millions of users provides it with a unique understanding of the intentions and interests of large sections of the global population. No organization has ever had access to such data either on such a scale or of such detail. Think about the searches you have run through your favourite search engine over the last month and what that says about you. It is not just search engines and social media companies such as Google and Facebook that are producing new types of information. Any organization that deals with large numbers of customers will be amassing details of transactions, purchases and other data from its operations. Business intelligence (BI) is used by large enterprises to try to gain competitive advantage from the manipulation of such internally generated data. BI systems from companies such as SAP and Oracle are transforming the ability of organizations to dig deeper into the information being spun off from their commercial activities, creating challenges for information analysts to make sense of what Bughin, Chui and Manyika (2010) call 'Big Data'. BI systems represent a new model of information production by the sheer scale of data they are generating and the level of detail about business operations they contain.

Our local supermarket, our credit card provider and the online retailer, Amazon, probably know more about many of us than our friends and family. Supermarket loyalty cards track what we buy, when we buy it and our responses to special offers and discounts. Matching this data with our address and combined with other data about our lifestyle that is easily accessible to the loyalty card operator provides a rich picture of how we live and what our interests are. Let's begin our exploration of new models of information production by entering the blogosphere and considering the impact blogs are having on magazine and newspaper industries.

Blogs and the challenge to publishers

At its heart a blog is simply a website with the content arranged in the order in which it was created with the most recent entries appearing first. The word blog is an abbreviation of weblog, which was first used in the late 1990s. The appeal of using a blog to post content to the web is its simplicity, with the blogger not requiring any knowledge of HTML coding or the technicalities of hosting a website. One of the first blogging platforms, Blogger, was launched in 1999 and the aspiring blogger now has a range of competing platforms to choose from including WordPress, Tumblr, TypePad and SquareSpace. Estimates for how many blogs there are vary enormously but the consensus seemed to be between 100 and 150 million by the end of 2010. However, this number will contain many abandoned blogs that their creators have long forgotten about and which exist in suspended animation in cyberspace. In the early days of blogging, critics were swift to characterize this new medium as a platform for lonely egotists to tell the world the dreary details of their lives. While there may have been some truth in this view, the last ten years have seen a number of blogs emerge as serious contenders to established print media in providing news editorial, entertainment and expert opinion. The Huffington Post in the USA and the Guido Fawkes' blog in the UK show how the blogging platform can challenge traditional journalism. During this period we have also seen mainstream media embrace blogging as a platform for their journalists to extend their commentary and supplement the outputs of newspapers, magazines and broadcasters. In the early days of blogging there was talk that this new medium represented a direct challenge to newspapers and would become a primary source of news for many people. However, the situation is more nuanced than one platform simply replacing another. New communication technologies seldom act as a straight replacement for another; television did not replace radio and mobile phones did not supplant fixed telephones.

The economics of print media

Producing newspapers and magazines is an expensive business and the market they operate in is viciously competitive. It is also becoming harder to make a profit as a print publisher, with sales of newspapers falling in many developed economies for several decades and new pressures emerging from the internet where many people do not expect to pay for their news. Graham and Hill (2009) outline some of the key challenges facing the newspaper industry and describe the approaches taken by publishers of regional newspapers to adapt to this new world of news. To better understand these challenges it is important to appreciate the key stages in the production of a newspaper. The value chain of printed news production is shown in Figure 2.1 where the main processes, actors, costs and revenues are highlighted.

The figure illustrates the range of costs that go into the production of a

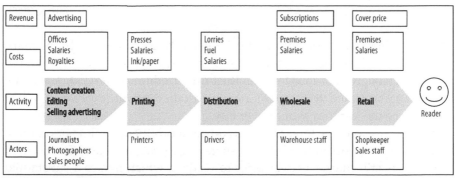

Figure 2.1 Traditional newspaper value chain

newspaper before it reaches the reader. Employing journalists, photographers and editors, buying printing presses and the ink and paper they require and then delivering the printed copies around the country to retailers and readers before breakfast is a costly and complicated enterprise. Unsold copies of a daily newspaper are worthless by the evening when the process of printing the next day's papers has already begun. The appeal to a publisher of the internet as a way to circumvent some of the processes is obvious. Figure 2.2, showing the more streamlined value chain of a news blog, illustrates this.

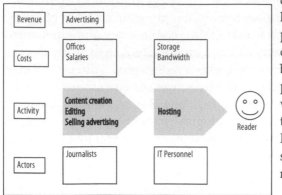

Figure 2.2 Value chain of a news blog

The impact on the cost structure of stripping out the printing and distribution of a newspaper will vary between publishers but it is possible it could save up to 60% of total costs (OECD, 2010). Jarvis, a veteran of print media and a prominent blogger, is critical of the approach taken by many news publishers in dealing with the internet and, slightly tongue in cheek, makes an ecological case for moving news online:

> Casting off atoms will allow newspapers to brag: no more dead trees and lost oxygen (an ecological site calculated that newsprint production used up the equivalent of 453 million trees in 2001); no more gas-sucking, pollution-spewing trucks to haul them around; no more presses draining energy; no more waste to recycle; no more oil pumped to make ink. To hell with going carbon-neutral. A former paper is an ecological hero!
>
> (Jarvis, 2009)

A world where news publishers no longer rely on paper as the primary medium for delivering their content may not be too far away. Jarvis (2009) recounts a talk given in 2005 by Alan Rusbridger, editor of the *Guardian* in the UK, where he stated the paper's newly installed printing presses would probably be the last they would ever buy.

However, despite the lower costs involved in producing online news there are also fewer opportunities for publishers to generate income. Most printed newspapers still charge a cover price to readers, which makes a substantial contribution to the overall revenue of the publisher. In Japan and much of

Europe, cover prices contribute over 50% to total newspaper revenues, with advertising making up the rest (OECD, 2010). Most US newspapers operate on a different revenue model with copy prices only averaging 13% of total revenues. While many people, albeit a declining number, are still prepared to pay for a printed newspaper there is less willingness to do the same for online news. Most online news sites have chosen to follow an advertising-based revenue model reflecting both the lower costs in news delivery as shown in Figure 2.2 but also the abundance of news related information that exists on the internet. Whereas printed papers are a limited resource for all the reasons that characterize physical media, a news website is only a click away resulting in a commodification of news and, it could be argued, a devaluing of this type of content. Some more specialist news providers, mainly those offering financial news, such as the *Financial Times* in the UK and the *Wall Street Journal* in the USA have managed to operate successful paywalls for their online content. However, the stories, commentary and analysis they offer is attractive to an audience with deeper pockets than most general news consumers. In 2010 News International began charging for online access to *The Times* and *Sunday Times*, its broadsheet UK titles. Despite many predictions that such a move would not attract sufficient subscribers, a year later there were some indications that it might be sustainable. According to Sabbagh (2011), 101,036 subscribers had signed up for a £8.67 monthly account leading him to conclude that there may be room for both free and paid-for online news providers.

So where do blogs fit into the news ecosystem and what impact are they having on the print media? The first thing to say is that, despite predictions to the contrary, news blogs have not replaced traditional news providers and are unlikely to do so in the near to medium terms. However, they are having an impact particularly in the area of specialist news normally provided by so called 'trade publishers'. In the USA, perhaps the most widely viewed and well known mainstream news blog is the Huffington Post, which offers its readers news and comment with a liberal leaning (see case study on page 19). The most popular of the Australian independent general news blogs is Crikey.com.au, which offers a website and subscription-based e-mail service. In July 2011, Crikey claimed it delivered over 2.5 million page impressions to 402,000 unique visitors, which compares quite favourably to Australia's highest circulation print newspaper, the *Sunday Telegraph*, which had a circulation of 618,000 in early 2011 (Jackson, 2011). While some news websites are attracting large audiences it is not clear to what extent they are contributing to the decline of print sales, which have been decreasing for several decades (OECD, 2010).

Other factors, including the popularity of television news and changing lifestyles, may also be significant. While there is no equivalent to Crikey or the Huffington Post in the UK, a number of newspapers have been keen adopters of blogs to extend their reach across the internet. All British newspapers have their own websites where stories and commentary from their print editions are reproduced but a number of them also give their journalists blogs which are embedded in the main news site. Blogging allows the print journalists to respond quickly to news stories and publish material that did not make it into print editions for space or editorial reasons. From the publisher's perspective this is an extremely cost-effective way of producing more content for their readers. Free from the restraints of print and paper, the reproduction costs of digital information is marginal. In September 2011, the *Guardian* website was hosting 60 blogs on subjects from technology, media and the environment to music, film and politics. The Guardian Environment blog, for example, has a core team of six bloggers plus other occasional contributors. One or two posts are added each day but it is the interaction with readers that generates the most information. Depending on the subject being discussed there will be varying levels of debate and discussion among commentators but 30 or more comments on a single post is not unusual. However, discussions are seldom on the scale seen on the Huffington Post, which is described in the case study below.

While a mainstream newspaper and a lone blogger may use the same platform to publish their writing to the internet, a key difference is that writers for newspapers are professional journalists while the lone blogger is often not. This does not necessarily mean the blogger's outputs are inferior but, for some people at least, they need to be seen in this context. Luckhurst, himself a former newspaper editor, feels strongly that amateur bloggers are not in the same league as their professional counterparts:

> The essential difference between the two deserves definition. It is that much blogging is an amateur activity carried out by people with no understanding of journalism's social purpose who operate with scant regard for facts.
>
> (Luckhurst, 2011)

Luckhurst may have a valid point if one is comparing a newspaper directly with a blog but perhaps this comparison is unfair. It might be argued that blogs should be seen as supplementary to the outputs of traditional news publishers and not as replacements. In this respect they are similar to podcasts; mainstream radio broadcasters still produce programmes but amateur podcasters have stepped in to fill some of the gaps for niche audiences as we will see later in this chapter.

CASE STUDY – THE HUFFINGTON POST

The Huffington Post was launched in the USA in 2005 as a news-based group-blog with content coming from a core team of journalists as well as contributions from over 3000 bloggers. In September 2011 Alexa, the web monitoring company, rated the Huffington Post as the 24th most visited website in the USA and 90th most visited site globally. According to Merced (2011) the site had revenues of $60 million in 2011. One of the reasons for the success of the Huffington Post is the way it engages with its readers and creates a community. Reader interaction is encouraged through the publishing of provocative stories and rewards such as the granting of virtual badges to active commentators. Helmore (2010) points out this engagement can be quantified by the 3 million comments the site's readers post each month. The comments section on news stories is more active than most other news sites, with a feature on President Obama attracting over 400 comments within an hour of it being posted on 23 October 2010. It is not unusual for an item on the site to attract over 5000 comments within a few days, far more than the websites of mainstream newspapers. In early 2011 the US internet and media company AOL bought the Huffington Post for $315 million, indicating to many that commercial businesses could be built around a blogging platform. On a smaller scale, the Guido Fawkes political news and gossip blog in the UK has been publishing satirical content since 2004 and in 2008 was listed by *The Economist* magazine as the country's most popular political blog.

Business publishing

If mainstream news is yet to be much impacted by the low-cost publishing revolution of blogs, more specialist news and information providers are feeling the pressure. This is particularly true with B2B (business to business) publishers, which produce information resources aimed at professionals working in the public and private sectors. These publications cater to very specific needs of IT (information technology), software buyers and people managing logistics functions such as shipping and road haulage. The titles of some of the publications in the B2B arena point to these specialisms: *Solicitors Journal, Pipeline and Gas Journal, Retail Week, Container Management, Floor Covering Weekly*. B2B publishers vary from very small operations that may produce only one or two very niche titles to large groups such as EMAP, Wolters Kluwer and Springer in Europe and Hearst Business Media and Penton Media in the USA. Traditionally, B2B publishing has been highly profitable as publishers have been able to deliver highly targeted audiences that often have high spending power to advertisers. If you are a producer of flooring products in the USA then *Floor Covering Weekly* is a key channel for reaching flooring contractors and distributors who make up the bulk of readers of this publication. Many B2B publishers will offer free subscriptions to qualified readers because the profit is in selling the advertising. However, as many business professionals move away from relying on specialist magazines as a source of information to using the internet, B2B publishing has, for many companies, become a lot less profitable. One of the reasons for this move away from print media is the opportunity that blogs and other websites allow industry experts to develop their own platforms for knowledge sharing and bypass the publishers. As a consequence and perhaps as a demonstration of a lack of confidence in the future of traditional B2B publishing a number of publishers including VNU, The Nielsen Company and Reed Elsevier have sold off their magazine businesses.

Recent research in Europe and the USA by PricewaterhouseCoopers highlights the challenges posed by the electronic delivery of information. In a survey of business professionals, many expressed a preference to obtain their information online. Similarly Fenez and van De Donk (2010) found that 60% of those surveyed visit a business website at least once a week. Although the PricewaterhouseCoopers research shows there is still demand for printed publications, the large B2B publishers now generate almost half their revenues through online activities. Fenez and van Der Donk see a long-term overall decline in the global advertising revenues of B2B publishers but believe that online advertising will increase as a proportion of the total at the expense of print advertising. The future, they argue, lies in publishers exploiting their valuable content and embedding their information services via live feeds and dynamic content into the workflows of their customers in a more active way than simply publishing magazines:

> The industry has moved on from simply being an aggregator of business-specific news. The priority now is to take advantage of all channels to become established as a trusted source of informed content. To do this and maintain their relevance, B2B publishers should be leveraging social networking trends.
>
> (Fenez and van Der Donk, 2010, 5)

A number of B2B publishers are starting to follow this advice by broadening their information portfolios and tapping into social networking technologies. In the scientific publishing sector, Nature Publishing Group offers podcasts and RSS feeds from its main website but its main innovation has been the Nature Network launched in 2007, which by December 2011 had attracted over 25,000 registered users. The Nature Network offers a free online space for scientists, students and other interested individuals to share information, discuss research and develop links across the scientific community in a similar way to more well known social networks such as Facebook and LinkedIn. All members of the network are given a blog, which provides a platform for individuals to promote themselves, their opinions and research to the broader community. For Nature Publishing Group this creates a valuable source of content, which they aggregate, track and index through a portal open to anyone surfing the web. As of December 2011 the Nature Network hosted more than 150 blogs with names ranging from 'Stripped Science' and 'Wonderland of Biophysics' to 'Confessions of a (former) Lab Rat' and 'The Art of Teaching Science'. While Nature Publishing Group shows how a traditional publisher in the scientific world can harness the power of online networks to complement its established businesses, examples of similar successful ventures in the business environment are rare. This might reflect the competitive nature of business where people are less willing to share information than in the more collaborative scientific communities. This could become an increasing problem for B2B publishers as they find themselves squeezed between large and established social networks such as LinkedIn and Facebook and the smaller, niche blogs and online communities that have no legacy print operations that impose cost burdens and restrict profitability. Whether this will lead to a transforming state of 'creative destruction' as described by Schumpeter (1950), whereby a new technology or set of technologies supplant an established way of doing business, remains to be seen. However, it is already the case that many print-centric B2B publishers which have not developed their web presence are becoming less relevant to their core audiences. David Gilbertson, chief executive of publisher Emap, describes how his business is responding to the digital challenge:

> The way I'd describe [the shift] is moving from the provision of information to providing intelligence. Companies like ourselves need to suggest what decision should arise, rather than just record that something occurred.
>
> (Bintliff, 2011)

Across a number of business sectors, web-based publishers such as Freepint, Sift and GigaOm (see case study below) are becoming trusted sources of information for professionals. LinkedIn Groups allow any LinkedIn member to create an online discussion group around a specific area of interest. By December 2011, LinkedIn hosted more than 1 million groups based around commercial areas such as telecommunications, advertising and human resources to non-profit and alumni interest groups. Membership ranges from over 500,000 members for the Human Resources Group down to several for more niche interests. These groups can be seen as shared blogs where questions are posted, answers given, polls run and opinions shared. Although some members use the groups to market themselves and their companies, they are undoubtedly an important source of valuable information for others. As such, they and the plethora of special-interest blogs that exist outside LinkedIn offer a new, more democratic channel for professionals to communicate and share information than was ever possible when traditional publishers dominated. Many of the large B2B publishers are aware of the increasing preference for online information delivery among their professional readers and have been active in developing online spaces to distribute their content. Perhaps indicative of the longer term future of paper as a medium for magazine publishing, Reed Elsevier, the UK's largest business publisher, decided in 2008 to sell off Reed Business Information, which produces a range of B2B titles. The failure to find a buyer and subsequent closure of a number of print titles possibly signals a terminal decline of what was once a highly profitable business model.

CASE STUDY – GIGAOM

GigaOm is a blog built on the WordPress blogging platform founded in 2006 by Om Malik, a US-based technology analyst, and offering expert commentary and analysis on a range of technology sectors. In December 2011 it was claiming over 4 million unique monthly visitors. Utilizing a range of contributors, GigaOM claims it 'is committed to bringing solid journalism to the web with a strategy that is grounded in the belief that media sites are no longer just publications, but rather hubs of business communities'. While the blog is free for anyone to access, GigaOm also offers a premium service allowing paying subscribers to access more detailed research and reports the company produces, accessible in a variety of digital formats such as PDF and HTML. GigaOm is not as large as more traditional publishers in this sector, such as Forrester or Gartner, but its $199 annual subscription cost is considerably less and presents an attractive alternative for small companies not able to afford the many thousands of dollars that larger competitors charge for similar information.

Wikis and collaborative publishing

The previous section showed some of the challenges facing traditional news and specialist publishers from the rise of new online sources of information, in particular blogs. While blogs present a definite challenge as well as opportunity to print publishers, they can be seen as an evolutionary development in information production in that, from the perspective of commercially driven blogs, there is still a formal editorial process and the need to generate revenues from advertising. Allied to this is the necessity for the people producing the content to be paid in some form or other. This section will consider another electronic challenge to print publishers in the form of the wiki as a publishing platform. Although wikis are more typically used as online collaborative platforms to share information within and across groups, the success of Wikipedia presents a revolutionary development in information production.

From a technical perspective, wikis differ from blogs in that they are a much more flexible platform for allowing users to add and edit content posted to the wiki site. In its most basic form, a wiki can be seen as a blank canvas on which users, depending on the permissions they have been given, can create pages and add text, links, images and other content. Another crucial feature of a wiki is that existing content can be edited and even removed by users. Where successfully deployed a wiki is a dynamic online space that reflects the needs and interests of its contributors without the constraints imposed by more structured content management systems such as blogs. While this flexibility may be seen as a strength of wikis, it could also be viewed as a weakness. The formal structure of a blog results in information being presented in a generally consistent manner that can be easily understood by its readers while, in theory at least, a wiki could be an anarchic collection of disparate and disorganized content. Wikipedia, however, demonstrates this need not be the case and shows how many thousands of contributors spread across the globe can create a trusted and valuable reference source for millions of internet users.

Created in the USA in 2001 by entrepreneur Jimmy Wales and philosopher Larry Sanger, Wikipedia, in March 2011, comprised over 19 million articles, is available in 278 languages and attracts over 400 million users a month, making it the world's 5th most popular website (www.wikipedia org/wiki/about). As part of the Wikimedia Foundation, in 2010, Wikipedia is sustained by fewer than 60 employees and has a budget of less than $5 million. Being able to maintain the creation of this much content along with the 12 million monthly edits that take place within Wikipedia would be impossible with this level of resources if it were not for the unpaid contributors who produce the information. While there is a relatively small core of unpaid 'Wikipedians' who oversee the production and editing of much of the site's content, most of the entries are open for any internet user to edit. Creating new pages is almost as easy but requires registration first, a free and straightforward process. With so few barriers preventing users from adding nonsensical or inaccurate information or from defacing the work of others it is, perhaps, not surprising that many commentators and educators were initially very sceptical about the veracity of Wikipedia and its value as a trusted reference source. Many schools and universities still prohibit students from citing Wikipedia in their work, although this seems to be changing as its value becomes recognized. A number of tests have been carried out to compare the accuracy of Wikipedia with more established reference sources.

Perhaps the most famous was in 2005 when the Nature Publishing Group compared a number of science-based entries between Wikipedia and Encyclopaedia Britannica and found little to choose between them in terms of accuracy. Although Encyclopaedia Britannica disputed the findings it was a watershed moment for Wikipedia and forced a number of sceptics to take a second look. Wikipedia would claim that what a number of critics see as its primary weakness is actually one of its key strengths: while almost anyone may add data to the site, the same people may also amend, edit and delete information they see as inaccurate or too trivial for inclusion. Working on the assumption that the number of people who care about creating and curating a valuable information resource outnumber those who would like to deface and undermine it, Wikipedia provides evidence of the power of collaboration.

Whatever the motives of those who contribute to this global experiment in information production, it is not financial and that could present a serious challenge to the business models of commercial publishers. For established publishers of encyclopaedias that is certainly the case. Encyclopaedia Britannica has been struggling since the early 1990s when competitors, particularly Encarta, started to offer encyclopaedias on CD-ROM. As personal computers started to appear in homes and on desktops these digital versions were particularly attractive in that they were easier to navigate, much cheaper, able to deliver multimedia and did not require the shelf space needed for the 32 Britannica volumes. While, in late 2011, it was still possible to buy the complete set of Encyclopaedia Britannica, at $1,395 the company is finding it very difficult to compete with the free and constantly updated Wikipedia. Not surprisingly, Britannica went online a number of years ago but has adopted a subscription model making it far less attractive to the mass of internet users who have grown up expecting information to be free and instantly accessible. Even Microsoft's Encarta encyclopaedia on CD-ROM, Britannica's first digital challenger, has given in to the challenge of Wikipedia and closed down in 2009 after 16 years of production.

The future for Wikipedia is not certain. While it is the single most popular source of reference information on the web and has proven that its volunteer model works in terms of producing generally accurate and valued information, it still requires income to operate. As the site carries no advertising and has no subscription model its revenues have been largely from donations. In 2010 the site launched a donation drive with a banner featuring the face of co-founder Jimmy Wales and his request for financial contributions. In its first month this raised over $50,000 but whether this will prove sufficient in the longer term remains to be seen. It is also worth noting that despite attempts to replicate the success of Wikipedia in other areas of information production, none have had nearly the same success. Wikipedia co-founder Larry Sanger launched a rival service, Citizendium, in 2007 but it never achieved critical mass. It is possible that such a venture only works where there is sufficient scale of interest in both producing and consuming the content. An encyclopaedia is by nature all-encompassing in its scope and so lends itself well to this distributed model of information production. Perhaps a sign that Wikipedia is gaining respectability, or at least acceptance, within the 'establishment' was a recent joint endeavour between the online encyclopaedia and the British Museum. The museum allowed a Wikipedia contributor and expert on antiquities to spend five weeks in the institution to help museum staff understand how Wikipedia works and show them how they can edit and improve content on the site. Acknowledging that Wikipedia is a starting point for many online researchers, the British Museum's head of web explained the initiative:

> . . . if we are going to accept that many people are going to use it to read about our objects [on Wikipedia], why not collaborate and make that article on Wikipedia as good as we can get it by working with them.
>
> (Hitchcock, 2011)

Search engines and what they know

While search engines such as Google and Bing are, for most people, the primary tool for finding information on the internet they also generate vast amounts of information in their own right. According to *The Economist* magazine (2010), every time we use a search engine and then click through the pages it serves up we leave a trail of 'data exhaust' behind us providing a rich source of information for marketers, academics and anyone else interested in human behaviour. In reference to Google, Battelle (2006) points out that the search giant is compiling a global 'database of intentions' built from the enquiries millions of us type into its search box every day. Before the mass adoption of the internet as an information resource, an understanding of the information needs and wishes of end-users was primarily confined to reference librarians. They were the focal point for enquiries by library patrons who could not locate the information they required by themselves. While directories, encyclopaedias and other reference sources were widely consulted by information seekers, the producers of these resources had no idea of the actual needs of those using them. Thousands of patrons may look for information in a library's directory of local businesses but their enquiries leave no trace once the directory has been closed and returned to the shelves. An internet search engine, on the other hand, maintains a log of the words people enter into the search box, allowing patterns of search behaviour to be observed and a deeper understanding of what people are most interested in.

Although there are a number of internet search engines freely available, Google is the dominant global player. Its market share varies between countries, from approximately 90% in the UK, to 60% in the USA and 20% in China. Although Google has extended its business into a number of other areas including mobile phones, ownership of YouTube, e-books and e-mail, 96% of its annual revenue in 2010 came from providing a platform for online advertising. By understanding from their search requests what it is that people are interested in, Google was able to generate $28.2 billion in 2010 from placing relevant advertisements next to its search results and relevant content on other websites. According to McGee (2010), in early 2010 Google was handling approximately 34,000 search queries per second, equivalent to 121 million per hour or 3 billion per day. This equates to more than 1 trillion searches a year giving Google a unique insight into what is on the minds of the 600 million people around the world who use the service on a regular basis.

While Google has been able to put this information to extremely profitable use with its Adwords programme, which places relevant online advertisements next to search results, third parties are also mining this new source of information for the insights it contains. Via Google Insights for Search, anyone can compare the frequency with which specific words and phrases are entered into the Google search box and then analyse how this varies over time and between geographic regions. For marketing professionals this can be useful as it allows comparisons of search activity between theirs and competing products. A comparison of 'coke' and 'pepsi' as search terms performed in December 2010 revealed, perhaps not surprisingly, 'coke' to be a moderately more popular search term than 'pepsi'. However, over the previous 12 months the country whose inhabitants had entered those terms the most had been Pakistan. This might be due to specific marketing activity for one or both those brands focused on that country and would certainly be of interest to management at the companies. Although this is a fairly trivial example it indicates the value that this 'data exhaust' has. Companies that sell products or services via their websites use this data to make sure they are including appropriate words on their sites. One of the variables that Google and other search engines take into account when presenting search results is how closely the keywords used on a website match the search terms a user has entered. If you sell mobile phones through your website, knowing the most popular words and phrases related to mobile phones that people are entering into Google allows you to optimize the text on the pages you want people to visit.

It is not just for marketing purposes that Google's 'database of intentions' offers value. Ginsberg et al. (2009) have used Google's search data to track the spread of influenza across the USA. By looking for patterns of certain keywords and phrases being typed in to the search engine they have been able to accurately estimate the rate of influenza levels in different regions of the USA. As people begin to feel ill with flu symptoms there are common words they type in to Google to look for health advice. This forms the basis of the predictive model developed by Ginsberg and his colleagues. The practical applications for such a model are significant in helping healthcare professionals and policy makers prioritize medical resources where they estimate they will be most needed. Similarly, politicians and their advisors have used search data to determine what issues voters are most concerned with in specific regions, allowing political messages to be tailored to particular localities.

While this new source of information offers a variety of opportunities for both commercial and public bodies, it also presents some challenges to informed decision making. Developing a better understanding of what your consumers, voters or patients are interested in can help develop better products and services. However, there is a danger it might stifle innovation by creating a feedback loop that encourages incremental innovations to what an organization does at the expense of more radical innovations. Many of the most important scientific and industrial breakthroughs did not come out of consulting the masses about what they wanted but emerged from the work of original thinkers and innovators. The technology underpinning the Google search engine itself was the result of mathematical research by two Stanford graduate students in the 1990s.

Our social graphs

Google's 'database of intentions' may have its finger on the pulse of what internet users are interested in but, for the most part, this data is fairly anonymous. One of the key technologies driving the so-called Web 2.0 revolution was social networking, which allowed us to forge virtual links with others online. MySpace and Friendster were two of the original social networking services but both have since been eclipsed by Facebook, which in December 2011 claimed to have more than 800 million active users, over a quarter of global users of the internet. Other social networks of note are the micro-blogging service Twitter and LinkedIn, which focuses on professional credentials, providing networking opportunities and a form of online CV. Like Google, they provide services that users value and for their owners they generate rich and valuable data about who is connected to who, what they are saying to each other and, through the groups they belong to and links they share, what their interests are. Facebook has copied Google to the extent that it presents advertisements which it considers will be of interest to its users. However, the method it uses to target these advertisements differs in that it draws on what it knows about its users. This information comes from the data we give Facebook about our age, gender, location, marital status, education and personal interests when we open an account. Advertisers are then able to construct advertising campaigns, which will be presented only to specific types of people. In itself this is a new source of information to the extent that no single organization has held this much data on the personal characteristics of so many people. The direct marketing industry has long made use of such data to help target their direct mail campaigns but it has had to rely on datasets of personal information from a range of providers, much of it out of date and inaccurate or based on generalized assumptions about the areas people live in. Facebook's database is far more dynamic, and is updated in almost real time by its users either directly or by their actions. For example, change your Facebook profile from married to single and you will probably start to see advertisements for dating agencies appearing on your pages. Change again from single to engaged and companies offering photographic services and other wedding-related offerings will appear.

This chapter is concerned with new models of information production and it could be argued that what Facebook has created is just a more sophisticated and larger database of personal information than has existed before. If this were all it had done then that might be a fair criticism. However, it is the addition of the social layer of information on top of this personal data that makes it unique. Knowing that Sarah is single, 31 years old, university educated and works as a nurse in the George Washington University Hospital in Washington DC is valuable information to the many companies and organizations that would like to communicate with her for commercial and non-commercial reasons. However, knowing this as well as who her friends are, what they talk about online, the Facebook groups she belongs to, web pages she 'likes', photos she has uploaded and events she has attended starts to build a complex and detailed picture of the person. Extend this level of detail across the 800 million plus users of Facebook and the argument that this is a new model of information production seems reasonable.

Apart from being able to help deliver more targeted advertisements to Facebook users, what is this data being used for? At the moment marketing is the main focus of commercial activity but a number of other applications are becoming apparent. Rosenbloom (2007) describes the value that this data has for social scientists interested in mapping and measuring how people communicate and interact online. She quotes Harvard sociology professor Nicholas Christakis on the potential of social media platforms for academic research: 'We're on the cusp of a new way of doing social science. Our predecessors could only dream of the kind of data we now have.' Christakis was this enthusiastic when Facebook only had 58 million active users; with more than ten times this number using the network in late 2011, the value to social scientists can only have increased. When a service like Facebook becomes so ubiquitous, it can almost be seen as a utility like water or the telephone network, which we take for granted and use unconsciously as part of our everyday lives. In this scenario it is possible to imagine it being used as a barometer for governments to gauge the mood of their citizens, a channel for important messages such as severe weather warnings to be distributed or just a place to locate and communicate with like-minded people. However, as well as these benign uses for Facebook's rapidly growing database, there is the obvious and much-discussed issue of privacy. Do we trust a company set up by a college student in 2004 with the often deeply personal data of hundreds of millions of people? Many don't and we will explore the privacy aspects of social networking later in this book.

So far this chapter has shown how internet-based services such as social media and online searching are producing new types of information that are being used by marketers to better understand our needs and desires. We have also seen how low-cost, easy to use self-publishing platforms such as blogs and wikis are impacting on more traditional publishers. The next section explores the emerging world of podcasting and podcasters and the challenge they present to the broadcasting world.

Podcasting and the democratization of the media

Before the mass take-up of the internet as an information sharing network, if you wanted to produce and distribute your own audio or video content you needed to own a radio or television network. Independent producers of such content existed but they relied on the established networks to commission and distribute their programmes. While these networks still produce and push out most of the audiovisual media that is consumed around the world, there are cracks starting to appear in the established order of big media. Podcasting and the technologies behind it are driving this change.

Podcasting emerged in the early 2000s as a way to push out audio recordings across the internet using the RSS standard for data distribution. This technology will be looked at in more detail in the next chapter but its importance in stimulating the production of audio and later on video programmes by independent producers is key. The ability of RSS feeds to handle audio attachments means that users can subscribe to audio programmes over the internet rather like programming a radio station into a radio. As new programmes are produced they are pushed out to subscribers and pulled into the software users have installed on their personal computers to read those feeds and decode the audio files such as iTunes or Winamp. In its early days this was a relatively technical process and required consumers to track down the podcasts that interested them, install the relevant software and then find a way to transfer the files to their audio or MP3 players. Web-based aggregators of podcasts began to appear very quickly as did search engines that focused on helping people find programmes of interest. However, it was the introduction of a podcast directory by Apple into its iTunes software in 2005 that gave this cottage industry its biggest boost. By this time iTunes and iPods had become the dominant software and hardware for individuals to manage their music collections. Allowing these users to subscribe, download and then synchronize their podcasts with their iPods via only a few clicks introduced podcasting to a non-technical audience. In the same year, video podcasts began to appear and become popular, as portable MP3 players offered video as well as audio playback.

While the outputs of the podcasting revolution are not new in terms of programmes being produced, it is the model of production that is novel. Independent producers now have a distribution mechanism at their disposal that bypassed the traditional network controllers. However, as with blogging, it is important not to see podcasting as a replacement for radio and television networks but rather a supplement to them. Indeed, some of the most popular podcasts are produced by 'old world' media organizations such as the BBC and Guardian in the UK and CNN and ABC in the USA. These large media companies use the time-shifting characteristic of podcasting to push out recordings of previously broadcast programmes as well as original programming often dealing with areas of specialist interest.

CASE STUDY – THE TWiT NETWORK

The TWiT network of audio and video programmes delivered via the internet was created in 2005 in the USA by Leo Laporte. Leo is an experienced radio and television presenter who saw the potential of the internet and podcasting technologies to allow independent producers like him to develop their own networks without the need for backing from traditional media companies or outside investors. Beginning with one audio podcast in 2005, This Week in Tech (TWiT), the network now employs a range of presenters and by late 2011 was producing 29 regular programmes, some of them streaming live over the internet on a daily basis. The network follows a hybrid commercial model of revenue generation mixing voluntary subscriptions with advertising inserted into the programmes. Amongst technology podcasts certain of the programmes are some of the most downloaded on the iTunes store, with approximately 5 million downloads a month. The TWiT network is interesting in that it shows a profitable media business can be created on the internet; according to Kalish (2010), the TWiT network generated $4 to $5 million in revenue in 2010. However, it also raises questions about the sustainability of such a business in terms of the ongoing running costs. Distributing large quantities of data across the internet is not free and media files tend to be the largest consumers of bandwidth. Unlike a traditional broadcast network that transmits via the airwaves, the costs of distribution of internet programming increase with every new listener. Where a network like TWiT is able to monetize its listeners through subscriptions and advertising this may not be a problem. However, podcasters that do not have commercial business models may find themselves losing money in direct proportion to the number of listeners they have. Although there is nothing in the UK quite on the same scale as the TWiT network, other organizations have adopted podcasting as a way to reach a broader audience. The *Guardian* newspaper, for example, offers podcasts on a range of subjects from arts to technology, while a small marketing agency based in Brighton, SiteVisibility, produces a weekly podcast on digital marketing, which has over 17,000 subscribers.

Podcasting, like blogging, may have reached a level of maturity in its life cycle as the initial hype concerning its potential to transform the media landscape has significantly diminished. Portable music players, whether standalone devices like iPods or smartphones, are now pervasive throughout the developed world and consumers are becoming more comfortable downloading podcasts and videocasts. Independent producers such as the TWiT network (see case study above) are emerging as the costs of the hardware and software necessary to produce quality programming decrease rapidly. However, the technology is only one part of the mix required to create media programming that people want to watch. The most important components are the creative and technical skills to think of and then produce the programmes. On top of this are the production costs; television series such as *Mad Men*, *Doctor Who* and *Lost* require significant financing. While such programming may be beyond the capabilities of small-scale podcasters, emerging technologies such as internet TV may disintermediate and thus pose a threat to the large television networks as the primary gatekeepers to our media consumption. The success of podcasting has shown there are both alternative producers of audiovisual content as well as demand from the general population for such materials. The following chapters will explore these changes in more detail from the distribution and consumption perspectives.

The challenge of big data

So far this chapter has considered new models of information production emerging from the internet and related technologies. Wikis, blogs, podcasts, search engines and social networking sites have become part of our everyday lives because the internet has provided an accessible platform for them. In the case of search engines and social networks we have seen valuable new datasets being created as by-products of the primary activity of those services. This final section will explore the challenges by organizations of all sorts as they struggle to make sense of the ever-increasing volumes of data they are generating through their everyday activities. Any organization, particularly those in the private sector, will be amassing data from its external interactions with suppliers, customers, competitors and regulators as well as internally from its employees and business processes. While companies have kept records of these transactions for centuries, what is new in the 21st century is the quantity and level of detail of this data as well as the ability to manipulate it for competitive advantage. According to senior IBM executive, Ambuj Goyal:

> In the past two or three years we have started to look at information as a strategic capital asset for the organization. This will generate 20, 30 or 40 per cent improvements in the way we run businesses as opposed to the 3 or 5 per cent improvements we achieved before. (Cane, 2009)

IBM has a vested interest in encouraging companies to spend more time and money on information management and analysis as it has spent billions of dollars building analytics centres and employing thousands of staff for this very purpose. However, the fact that organizations have never generated so much data is not in doubt and neither is the growing recognition that developing an understanding of what it all means is increasingly important. It has been estimated that some of the experiments at the Large Hadron Collider at CERN near Geneva generate over 40 terabytes of data a second, far more than can currently be analysed. On a smaller but still significant scale, a typical large supermarket chain will sell tens of billions of items a year to millions of customers across hundreds of stores. For example, UK supermarket chain Tesco has over 15 million users of its Clubcard loyalty scheme, which processes approximately 6 million transactions a day. According to Davey (2009) each of these transactions produces 45 different data points requiring Tesco to process over 270 million variables every day as it attempts to make sense of the data its stores are generating. As information technology became embedded in organizations, the volume of data being generated by companies is estimated to be doubling every 12 to 18 months. Davenport, Harris and Morison (2010) argue that this data has real value not only to the organization collecting it but also to third parties that can make use of it. Davenport cites the case of a US supermarket chain, which made more money selling its internally generated data to a retail data syndication firm than it did selling meat. The company then went on to admit it made little use of the data beyond putting it on tape, storing it in a mountain and making sure it was safe from nuclear attack (Davenport, Harris and Morison, 2010, 89).

The growth of these massive, internally generated data sets presents a number of challenges to information professionals, particularly those working in the corporate sector. Traditionally their work has been to manage information that originated from outside their organization, produced by third party publishers. However, the skills needed to classify, organize and disseminate external information do not often translate well to managing data sets of the sort described above. Expertise in computer programming and statistical analysis are often more useful and it is an area that library and information courses might consider incorporating into their curricula. Bentley (2011) believes that organizations are struggling to find the information they need within their own data sets and that information professionals are often those put under pressure to solve this problem. While some new technical capabilities may be needed to address this challenge, many library and information professionals already possess the core skills, according to Hyams (2011a). An understanding of the principles of classification is key to being able to grasp what the issues for the organization are. Quoting Vanda Broughton, an expert in classification and indexing, Hyams makes the case for traditional library and information courses,

> . . . suddenly, there's an overwhelming amount of information. You might not be able to put structure into it, but having a structured approach, understanding what the problems might be, are really important. It's important to teach [classification] in some depth, because it's only by doing it in some depth that you see why it really matters.
>
> (Hyams, 2011a, 23)

Data types

So what are the types of data which organizations are collecting to create these new datasets? They can be divided into two broad types: structured and unstructured. Structured data typically emerges from transactions that an organization takes part in, such as the purchase and sales of goods. Most products a retailer sells will have their own unique identifier in the form of a barcode and number. This is used to track the products from their delivery to a central warehouse, then to a specific store and finally through the checkout when a customer buys it. At the point of sale in many stores the sale of the product will be linked to a customer's loyalty card, which allows the retailer to better understand the purchasing habits of its shoppers. In the case of large retailers such as Tesco in the UK and Walmart in the USA, the data is collected in near real time with billions of rows of information added to their datasets every day, according to Babcock (2006). Being able to visualize this much data is difficult and so comparisons with a tangible information artefact is useful. It is estimated that Walmart manages approximately 3 petabytes of data which, according to Lyman and Varian (2003) would be equivalent to the contents of 22 US Libraries of Congress or 374 million books. Bearing in mind that this data is changing on an hourly basis, making sense of it and using it to make strategic business decisions presents a challenge. However, there are companies specializing in data analysis that can do this, drawing on the power of supercomputers to do so. At a relatively mundane level these analyses might help the retailer think about where to position products in a store, based on previous sales and configurations. At a more strategic level they might provide insights into where new stores should be established and help with international expansion. As organizations of all sizes and across many sectors continue to create these new forms of information as by-products of their operations, companies providing the software and hardware to process it are also expanding to the extent that Bhattacharjee (2010) expects the market for such services to be worth $13 billion by 2013.

The above examples relate to the generation of fairly structured sets of data that, scale apart, can be processed relatively easily by computers and the software running on them; products and consumers can be given unique identifiers allowing the tracking of purchases and sales. However, a more recent type of information that organizations are having to understand is less structured and comes in the form of e-mails, recorded phone calls both into and out of the organization, as well as the chatter about their products and services that takes place on the internet. It is this latter type of information that presents some of the greatest challenges, as what people say about you or your company is often beyond your control. Web-based services such as Alterian SM2 and Radian6 allow subscribers to monitor mentions of specific companies, products and brands across a range of social media in much the same way that press clippings agencies have done through the scanning of newspapers. The main difference between these new services and the press clippings agency is the response times. While press clippings may have been delivered on a monthly, weekly or even daily basis, social media monitoring services operate in almost real time and companies with reputations to forge and protect will often respond as quickly. As some major brands have discovered, ignoring the online conversations where criticisms are voiced is often not a good idea. Word of mouth takes on a new meaning when applied to social media and the way messages spread virally. Dell found this out to its cost in 2005 when a dissatisfied, high profile blogger, Jeff Jarvis, wrote about his frustrations in trying to have his faulty computer replaced by the manufacturer. His comments struck a chord with the readers of his blog and comments started to be posted about others' experiences of Dell's customer service. Eventually Dell did respond and dealt with the faulty computer but not until adverse publicity had, according to Weber (2009), cost the company hundreds of thousands of dollars in lost business and damage to its reputation. Using social media monitoring tools such as those mentioned above, many companies now try to keep track of what current and potential customers are saying about them and, where they can, try to add their voice to the conversations. As corporate and brand images become harder to manage and the traditional marketing model of central control is weakened by the decentralized nature of the internet, organizations will have to devote more time to engaging online with their customers.

Concluding comments

This chapter has considered how new technologies, in particular mass computing and the internet, are leading to new models by which information is produced. These are challenging some established business sectors such as publishing and broadcasting but also presenting new opportunities for innovation and business creation. As the technologies that are leading these changes become cheaper and more widespread, their effects will be magnified. The next chapter will explore the next stage in the information value chain and look at the new ways we are storing information and some of the challenges they present to information professionals, traditionally the guardians of such assets.

QUESTIONS TO THINK ABOUT

1. What are some of the defining characteristics of the internet and world wide web that have stimulated the creation of new models of information production?
2. What are some of the current and potential commercial conflicts that these new models engender?
3. What are some of the challenges that these new models present to information professionals?
4. Are the traditional skills of the library and information professional relevant in this emerging world of digital information?

CHAPTER 3
New models of information storage

Introduction

Societies that had no way of codifying information relied on the human memory and story-telling as the only way to share information and to pass it down to future generations. A number of myths and legends that are now part of our literature and culture are likely to have originated from what is called the oral tradition. By the nature of such memorized story-telling it is often impossible to ascertain where stories originate but it is likely that the legend of Beowulf as well as the poems of Homer started life in this way. The development of the cuneiform writing system over 5000 years ago and subsequent alphabets that we would now recognize enabled information to be transcribed for the first time and provided one of the cornerstones for the emergence of what we would call civilization. Financial imperatives drove much of the innovation in writing methods as traders needed to document their purchases and sales and public officials took note of taxes which were due or had been paid. That we know anything about these early alphabets is due to many of them being written into clay tablets, which have lasted through the millennia. Apart from the development of new media such as parchment and paper for storing texts, the evolution of writing tools such as pencils and pens and then the invention of the printing press to make the reproduction of documents more efficient, little else has changed since the first clay tablets of 3000 BC. Of course, the inventions mentioned above were significant, particularly the printing press, but the final output was always the same: a physical, analogue representation of the information. While typewriters and printing presses allowed books, newspapers and other documents to be created at ever lower costs and in larger numbers, what came out of the machine was still something with weight and volume that degraded over time and required physical space to be stored. Much of the work of librarians over the last several hundred years has been the management of these physical resources, which has of course required shelving, storage repositories and the replacement and rotation of stock as it wears out or becomes outdated. Digital information is not subject to many of these limitations as it has no significant physical footprint and does not wear out in the traditional sense. However many times a digital document is read, copied and shared the integrity of its content is not impaired.

Apart from printed formats, information has been stored in other analogue formats such as phonograph cylinders, gramophone records and audio and video tapes. However, like books these storage media took up considerable physical space and, unlike digital formats, were subject to degradations in quality and integrity the more they were copied. With the advent of the first computers in the 1940s, one of the primary aims of computer scientists was to develop new ways of storing the data that the computers required for processing as well as their outputs. Punch cards similar to those previously used by player pianos and weaving looms of the 19th century were the primary storage medium for computers until replaced by magnetic tape and then the disc drives we are familiar with today. The early computers of the 1950s weighed hundreds of kilograms, cost millions of pounds in today's money and could store less than a three-thousandth of the data held in a standard smartphone of 2012. Apart from increases in the capacity of modern computer storage, the fall in price is equally dramatic: a megabyte of storage in the mid-1950s cost approximately £120,000 in today's money while a megabyte in 2012 costs less than 0.005 pence. As Levie (2011) points out, by 2020 businesses will have to deal with 50 times the amount of data they do in 2011 and 'Our software, infrastructure, and organizations are ill-prepared to manage this scale of data creation, let alone generate anything meaningful or useful with this amount of content being created and shared.' This chapter will explore the implications of these changes for the way we manage information in the 21st century and what it means for the organizations and individuals that produce and consume the ever-increasing streams of digital bits.

Preserving the internet

Over 2000 years ago the Great Library of Alexandria held the greatest collection of manuscripts ever gathered from around the world. It was a bold attempt to capture the knowledge of the ancient world through recognition of the power of codified information. Phillips (2010) points to the aggressive acquisition strategy of the library's keepers that eventually led to a collection of between 400,000 and 700,000 items. As significant as the unprecedented size of the library itself are the tales of its destruction. How the Great Library and its many scrolls and books eventually met their end is a matter of debate but their disappearance is not. Either through fire, vandalism or theft, this priceless collection was lost to the world, never to be reassembled again. Parallels have been drawn with the internet and the, often transient, information that is dispersed across web servers around the world.

In many countries, publishers are legally obliged to deposit at least one copy of every book and magazine they produce with public repositories, often the national library. Until very recently this has resulted in comprehensive archives of mainstream printed materials and given us a series of modern-day equivalents of the Great Library of Alexandria. However, the rise of digital forms of information have presented challenges to these endeavours. The web as a publishing platform makes the creation of a single repository for publications almost impossible. Web pages are particularly transient and often have a very limited life-span. Dellavalle et al. (2003) point out the dangers of relying on the permanence of web links when referencing materials. Their research in the USA showed that almost 20% of the URLs used in a high school science curriculum became inactive between August 2002 and March 2003. Much of the value we derive from the web is based on the free linking between information resources but this is also a fundamental weakness as websites can be taken down as easily as they were created in the first place. As new web formats emerge such as blogs, wikis and other content management publishing systems, keeping track of who is publishing what and preserving their outputs is increasingly difficult. In the 1990s when the web was still in its infancy, Yahoo!'s directory of websites based around subject areas was the starting point for many researchers seeking information. This subject-based approach to organizing the web may seem rather quaint now but it was a useful resource when websites were counted in the hundreds of thousands and not the hundreds of millions as they are today. In 2010 Yahoo! closed its European directory sites as it became impossible to update and maintain such resource-hungry operations, although it claims a commitment to the US Yahoo! directory (Schwartz, 2010). Although Yahoo! in the USA and the still functioning, as of late 2011, DMOZ open directory project do not host websites themselves they do provide a snapshot of significant web resources. However, as web pages disappear they provide no backup of those resources in the way that a national archive does. Although books go out of print we are usually able to locate a copy in the British Library, the Library of Congress or whatever institution in our country is charged with maintaining such a resource. Is anyone doing the same for the internet?

Luckily for those concerned about the disappearance of web pages the answer is a qualified yes. Since 1996 the Internet Archive in the USA has been archiving websites and making them available to internet users through its Wayback Machine, a freely accessible resource that allows anyone to look at previous versions of websites. The Internet Archive is a non-profit organization and has no legal rights to oblige owners of web pages to lodge copies of their materials with it. However, with the support of grants and donations from individuals and charities it has amassed the world's largest repository of web pages. According to its own website in December 2010, it had collected almost 2.4 petabytes (approximately 85 billion web pages) of information spread across four data centres and this was growing at a rate of 100,000 gigabytes of information a month. The driving force behind the Internet Archive is Brewster Kahle who, although not a librarian by profession, embodies some of the key characteristics of any successful library and information professional. He was even described in a 2009 article in *The Economist* magazine as 'the internet's librarian' (Economist, 2009). Kahle himself draws parallels between his archive and the Great Library of Alexandria in terms of their objectives, with the Internet Archive making the following claim on its 'About' page:

> Libraries exist to preserve society's cultural artefacts and to provide access to them. If libraries are to continue to foster education and scholarship in this era of digital technology, it's essential for them to extend those functions into the digital world.   (Internet Archive, 2011)

Despite its best endeavours, however, the Internet Archive can only ever offer snapshots in time of the state of the web with many pages never being indexed because they were changed before the archive visited them, were never found in the first place or lay behind password-protected firewalls. It is inevitable that much of what is published on the web will never be preserved and will disappear into digital darkness. While it could be argued that much of this lost information was of such a trivial nature that its demise will be no loss to humanity it could equally be said that what seems trivial and unimportant now may have a significance to future generations that we cannot yet comprehend. It is often the diaries of everyday folk or informal personal photographs that tell us more about our past than official records. Although the Internet Archive is an attempt to capture web resources on a global scale it should be noted that a number of smaller, more local initiatives are under way to build digital archives, and some of these are considered later in this chapter.

The Internet Archive is a public-spirited attempt to store digital information for the benefit of current and future generations and maintains a significant technical infrastructure to securely hold this information. However, in the for-profit sector there are far larger investments being made to capture and store the data that drives the web. As the world's most popular search engine, Google is at the forefront of these attempts to index the web. Google is reticent about releasing data on its operations, but in 2008 the company revealed on its official blog that it was indexing more than 1 trillion pages, 1000 times larger than the index of 1 billion pages it created in 2000 (Alpert and Hajaj, 2008). Underpinning Google's operations are approximately 900,000 servers consuming an estimated 0.01% of the world's electricity (Miller, 2011). Finding low-cost and reliable sources of energy to power and cool its data centres is an ongoing challenge for Google, which is investing hundreds of millions of dollars in solar and wind farms, as well as building centres next to the sea and in the Arctic Circle where cooling can be done naturally. While Google manages the most web servers, other internet companies are not too far behind in their requirements for computer storage. Facebook's more than 800 million users had by late 2011 uploaded more than 30 billion pieces of content such as photos, posts and notes.

How organizations store information

The previous section examined how the Internet Archive and Google are attempting, for different reasons, to store web pages and associated data on a global scale. This section moves down to the organizational level and considers how our public and private bodies are managing their digital data. As most of the information that we deal with in our daily work lives is becoming digital it is a growing challenge for organizations to manage it in a way that is secure, compliant with legal requirements and readily accessible to employees, regulators and other stakeholders as and when they need it. Information has moved out of filing cabinets and bookshelves and onto personal computers, file servers, memory sticks, smartphones and content management systems.

Academia

Universities and colleges of higher education have long been one of the primary producers of original research materials that have been the basis for many world-changing innovations. The founders of Google, Larry Page and Sergey Brin, were students at Stanford University in the USA when their research project involved the creation of a web crawler that formed the foundation of the Google search engine. The key channels for disseminating academic research findings are the peer reviewed journals that cover academic disciplines from archaeology to zoology with titles such as *Celestial*

Mechanics and Dynamical Astronomy and *The Journal of Phenomenological Psychology*. While these journals are still the primary method for academics to present their research there is a trend for academic institutions to host their research outputs in their own online institutional repositories (IRs) that are accessible via the internet.

In a world where anyone with an internet connection can distribute their own digital content without the need for editorial control and the permission of an established publisher, it seems logical that universities should also be able to join in. Peer reviewed journals and conference proceedings are often expensive for users to access and prevent potentially useful information gaining a wider distribution. This has encouraged the deployment of institutional digital repositories by many universities (see case study below), which are making research findings accessible over the public web. Lynch (2003) in Heery and Powell (2006) offers a broad but useful definition of what he sees as the key characteristics of an IR:

> a university-based institutional repository is a set of services that a university
> offers to the members of its community for the management and dissemination
> of digital materials created by the institution and its community members. . . . An
> institutional repository is not simply a fixed set of software and hardware.
>
> (Heery and Powell, 2006)

For academic librarians, the development of IRs presents both challenges and opportunities. Some of these challenges centre on the acquisition and maintenance of new technical skills required to help specify, design and implement these new systems. The nature of their core skills in managing information means librarians are well placed to play an active role in these tasks. However, as with the deployment of other technical innovations across organizations, there is the potential for tension between library and information professionals and IT staff over who is responsible for making key decisions. Newton, Miller and Stowell Bracke (2011) describe the skills required by academic librarians to lead the deployment of IRs and argue that such information professionals may indeed 'find themselves building or strengthening relationships with disciplinary faculty and research centres on campus while extending the boundaries of library service' (Newton, Miller and Stowell Bracke, 2011).

Once the IR is up and running the next task is to keep it populated with the latest research outputs from academic researchers in the institution. As with many content management systems in all types of organizations, this is an ongoing challenge. Assuming that because a system has been set up to hold research materials it will automatically be used in that way is a mistake.

Without the right incentives most people will not be inclined, for reasons of time or plain laziness, to upload materials. Carrot and stick approaches can be used to encourage positive behaviours. Carrot approaches might be to demonstrate to users the benefits of having their outputs exposed to a wider audience or offering rewards for regular uploaders. A more stringent stick might be applied in the form of contractual obligations to place materials on the IR or the withholding of research funding for non-compliance.

It is worth noting that one of the advantages an IR offers over the traditional academic publishing model is the variety of file types and formats it can hold. While the peer-reviewed journal paper is still the gold standard for evaluating the work of an academic, an IR allows other types of outputs to be stored and distributed to a wide audience. These may include working papers, presentations, videos and original data sets. There is of course a danger of the IR containing too much trivial information and this is where the skills of the information professional may be needed to sift through the noise of digital artefacts and find the nuggets of valuable information. Just as Google, through its PageRank algorithm, has helped internet users find the information they need from hundreds of millions of websites, so new tools such as OAIster and Google Scholar are being developed to index and help people find the academic outputs they require from IRs (Stevenson and Hodges, 2008). It will be increasingly important for IRs to be found and indexed by such services if they are to remain visible and relevant to the research community. The use of common file formats and readable metadata play an important role in this respect as does the cooperation between academic institutions, research funding bodies, search companies and publishers. Woodward and Estelle (2010) point out that as long as the IR complies with the Open Archives Initiative Protocol for Metedata Harvesting (OAI-OMH), any item should be discoverable by commonly used web search engines.

CASE STUDY – UNIVERSITY OF SOUTHAMPTON E-PRINTS INSTITUTIONAL REPOSITORY

The University of Southampton is one of the top research institutions in the UK and teaches more than 17,000 undergraduate and 7000 postgraduate students. The university was one of the first in 2003 to develop an institutional repository which was built using open source software developed within the university. By 2008 it held over 3000 items and this had grown to over 60,000 by late 2011. Users can search using an advanced interface or browse the collection, which is organized by Library of Congress subject areas. To encourage academics to deposit their research, in 2006 the university instigated a policy that all staff should at least deposit bibliographic information of all their research outputs and, where possible, upload post-prints of journal and conference papers. The open pource software powering e-prints was developed by the University of Southampton and is one of the most widely used pieces of repository software in the world, with users including the Open University in the UK and the California Institute of Technology (Caltech) in the USA. One of the key attractions of e-prints is, because it is open source, the ability of users to customize and configure the software in a way that suits their needs.

The private sector
Just as academic institutions are exploiting cheap data storage and an open web to share the outputs of their research to a wider audience, so too are private enterprises building large-scale data centres to house a wide range of digital information. These data centres may be used for reasons of competitive advantage and/or for legal requirements where data retention is important to comply with financial legislation. The scale of some of these initiatives is forcing innovations in data security, storage capacity and energy use.

Legal requirements
Until recently it was generally public bodies that were legally required to maintain records for fixed periods of time. This information was typically the outputs of administrative bodies as they carried out the work of the executive and legislative parts of government. In the UK the Public Record Office Act of 1838 was passed to 'keep safely the public records' and has been amended over the years, most recently in 2010 with the Constitutional Reform and Governance Act. Similar legislation exists at state and national levels across most developed economies where obligations are placed on public bodies in terms of how long data must be retained, as well as the access rights to those documents by the general public. Over the last several decades legislation on document retention has also extended to private companies, a trend that has accelerated since 2000 following financial scandals and fears over terrorist activities.

In the USA the collapse of Enron and WorldCom, and other corporate failures due to financial malpractice in the late 1990s and early 2000s, led the US Congress to pass the Sarbanes-Oxley Act (SOX), which placed more stringent financial accounting obligations on publicly quoted companies. As well as applying to US corporations it also extends to foreign-owned companies that have listings on the US stock market. The Act has been criticized by many companies because of the increased costs it imposes on them through compliance with the new accounting rules as well as through the obligation for public companies to store internally generated information for periods of up to seven years. According to Kidd (2003) there are over 10,000 separate laws in the USA that deal with document and data retention but SOX is the most onerous in terms of the obligations it places on companies. In the UK, the data consulting firm, Watson Hall (2009) lists 37 different types of data that organizations, public and private, are required to retain for periods of between four days and 50 years, and in some cases indefinitely. The types of data described by Watson Hall include e-mails, personnel records, web activity and telephone records. Some of this information will be in paper format and stored in the traditional sense but increasingly it will be digital, requiring new skills and procedures on the part of those responsible for its maintenance. Where information is paper-based there are physical objects that cannot be ignored and, in some respects, their retention is easier than less tangible digital data. Accidentally wiping a hard disc drive is easily done so procedures need to be in place to maintain audits of electronic information along with instructions for backing it up to secure locations. The fragility of digital data was highlighted in 2007 when a computer technician from the Alaskan tax office accidentally erased a disc drive containing an account worth US$38 billion while doing routine maintenance work (Maxcer, 2007). When the tape backups of the data were found to be unreadable, staff in the department had to rescan and enter data stored in over 300 cardboard boxes, which cost $200,000 in overtime payments. Although this example may be at the extreme end of data storage problems, it illustrates both the temporal nature of digital data and the value of paper backups. However, for most organizations maintaining both forms is not practical.

While SOX in the USA and other similar legislation around the world are aimed at preventing illegal accounting practices in the corporations, other legislation has been enacted in the wake of terrorist activities in the USA and Europe. These are having implications for telephone and internet companies and forcing them to store ever-increasing amounts of information about their customers for longer periods of time. After the 2001 attacks on New York City and Washington DC and the 2005 bombings in London there was a concern that telephone and e-mail communications between the attackers were not being stored by internet and telecommunications providers to allow investigations by the security services. In Europe this has been driven by the European Union Data Retention Directive (EUDRD) of 2006 and in the USA by the Patriot Act of 2001. Both these pieces of legislation place responsibilities on telecommunication and internet service providers (ISPs) for keeping customer records and providing access when required to official bodies. In the UK the EUDRD has been enacted in a way that puts the responsibility for storing and managing all internet communication data with the ISPs themselves. Data must be stored for at least six months and no longer than two years (Pauly, 2009). While this may seem sensible for reasons of national security, the implications for the ISPs and telecommunications operators is considerable. The media regulator Ofcom estimates that in 2010 in the UK over 250 billion minutes of voice conversations were carried across the networks, 130 billion texts were sent and over 1 trillion e-mails exchanged on top of over 600 million gigabytes of web traffic (Ofcom, 2011). The logistics for the carriers of having to store details of those communications, including every website that a customer visits, for up to two years, is considerable. In Austria it was calculated that the cost to ISPs of compliance with the EUDRD could be up to 20 million euros a year, a considerable sum for companies operating in a highly competitive market (Libbenga, 2011).

Apart from the issues surrounding personal privacy of such granular data being stored and the costs mentioned above, the logistics of storing such massive volumes of data in a format that allows it to be searched and possibly retrieved on demand is presenting substantial technical challenges. Active discussions around the world are taking place between politicians, regulators and communications companies as to how national and international pieces of legislation should be enacted and these are likely to continue for the foreseeable future. While storing such information is seen by many organizations as a burden that reduces profits, a large number of businesses are investing large sums to build databases for purely commercial reasons. The following section considers the growth in data mining that is driving attempts to better understand customer behaviour and many of the other variables that affect business performance.

Data mining

In Chapter 2 we saw that as companies generate ever-increasing amounts of data from their operations they increasingly see these new information streams as sources of competitive advantage. Retailers are a good example of this trend where large supermarkets such as Tesco in the UK and Walmart (see case study below) in the USA will typically sell thousands of product lines to millions of customers every day. Keeping track of these transactions is essential to make sure that products are replaced on the shelves in a timely manner but the data generated also provides some valuable insights into customer behaviour, which can help increase sales and profits.

CASE STUDY – WALMART

Walmart, founded in the USA in 1962, is the world's largest retailer and operates more than 8500 stores around the world, which trade under a range of names;

Asda is its UK chain of supermarkets. In 2010 it had revenues of $418 billion, a gross profit of $104 billion and was valued by the New York Stock Exchange at $185 billion. One of the key factors in its success is the company's ability to capture, store and analyse vast amounts of data relating to the products it sells and the customers who buy them. According to Babcock (2006), the company is moving towards real-time capture and analysis of sales information with billions of rows of data being added to the database every day. Walmart does not often release details of its technology infrastructure but in 2006 Babcock claims that it was storing over 580 terabytes of sales and inventory data spread over more than 1000 computers in its data warehouses. In 2012 these figures are likely to have grown considerably as the company expands it data centre operations; during 2011 plans were under way for a new $100 million data centre in Colorado spread over 23 acres of land. So what does Walmart do with all this information? By looking for trends and patterns in what customers buy, at what time and in what stores, the company's data analysts can help store managers adjust prices and move products around the stores to increase sales. Small changes to stock pricing and location on shelves when implemented across thousands of stores have had a significant positive impact on the profitability of Walmart over the last 20 years. Chen and Chen (2007) argue that similar analysis of stock purchase, display and rotation in libraries can also have a positive effect on increasing usage by local communities.

The large data centres being built by some of the global internet companies such as Google and Amazon were described earlier in this chapter but it is important to note that companies of all sizes are placing greater emphasis on the value of their data assets. Large retailers such as Walmart and Tesco provide obvious examples of this trend but it also applies to smaller companies that can leverage their data to compete more effectively. One of the constraints facing small and medium enterprises (SMEs) has been the cost of managing data centres and the lack of knowledge of what to do with the data once it is captured. Just as the internet has made it easier for new entrants to the retail sector to compete with established players through e-commerce, so too is the same technology providing new sources of data to evaluate and low-cost tools to perform the analysis. Budnarowska and Marciniak (2009) show how a free tool such as Google Analytics can help small online retailers better understand how visitors to their websites behave and the factors that lead to actual sales. Other low-cost online tools such as Salesforce.com and Insightly also offer powerful applications for customer relationship management (CRM) that have previously been the domain of large companies. One of the key differences apart from the price is that the data is not stored by the companies themselves but is accessed via the internet and managed by the service providers. This cloud-based approach to application and data access is allowing SMEs to use data management services that were previously unaffordable.

Figure 3.1 is a simplified version of the key stages involved in data mining and can be applied across a range of organizational types. While the focus of data mining activities has traditionally been in the commercial sector and security services, it also has relevance to many public organizations including libraries of all types. Just as a retailer is concerned with maximizing efficiencies in the way it purchases, displays and sells stock so too libraries need to ensure they hold the titles their patrons want, in sufficient quantities and in the right locations. While a local library service is not going to have the same budget for these activities as Walmart or Tesco, there are ways it can engage in understanding customer data that don't cost the earth. Broady-Preston and Felice (2006) describe some tentative steps taken by the University of Malta library service to develop better relationships with the users through a CRM system, with mixed results. Wang (2007) points to resistance on the part of staff in implementing a CRM system in an academic library but describes the benefits that can accrue if the system is carefully thought through. Libraries are certainly able to generate enough data on their operations and customers to populate a CRM system including data on stock held, items loaned, activity of users, loan lengths, as well as activity on their websites. With financial pressures on library staff, public and academic, likely to increase over the coming years, developing a better understanding of users, their habits and requirements will become a more important task. Maintaining and analysing records of these activities and preferences will play an important part in this.

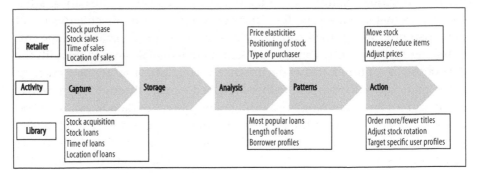

Figure 3.1 Data mining activities for retailers and libraries

Collection digitization

The CRM activities described above will play an increasing role in the jobs of many library staff and put pressures on the data they are required to store but it is the collections they manage and provide access to that will always be at the core of their responsibilities. Woodward and Estelle (2010) point out that although Google is probably the single largest creator of digital assets through its Google Books project and other initiatives, individual libraries are also actively engaged in digitizing their collections. They describe the US Library of Congress's $2 million project to digitize old, brittle books and the £22 million digitization programme funded by JISC in the UK that encompasses old sound recordings, newspapers and cartoons.

In the UK the British Library has been active in creating and offering access to digital versions of its printed collections. By late 2011, the library was offering access via its website to over 4 million digital items and 40 million pages (British Library, 2011). In a sign of the inevitable move to digital content creation and curation, the chief executive of the British Library, Dame Lynne Brindley, said in 2010:

> By the year 2020 we estimate that only 25% of all titles worldwide will be published in print form alone. 75% will only be published digitally, or in both digital and print form. Our research suggests that as use of mobile devices become ubiquitous, users will expect seamless access to information and services, and will assume that everything is available on the web.
>
> (Guardian, 2010)

As well as preparing for the storage of future digital content, the British Library is also creating digital versions of much of its analogue archive of books, newspapers, magazines and other collections. In June 2011 it announced a joint project with Google to digitize 250,000 out of copyright books, pamphlets and periodicals from the period 1700 to 1870. This and other digitization projects by the British Library are presenting significant challenges to its technical infrastructure in terms of being able to store and then provide access to the archive content. In order to maintain the security of the archives all content is mirrored across two sites so that if one site was to suffer a disaster the other would hold a copy of the many hundreds of terabytes of data so far collected.

Digitizing collections offers many advantages to both the curators and those looking for information across the archives. Space savings and the absences of worries about the effects of time and humidity on paper resources are obvious benefits as is the ease with which digital collections can be indexed and searched. However, while paper and ink are universally accessible and readable forms of information representation that are capable of lasting centuries under the right conditions, digital files may not be so robust. It is understood that digital storage media such as hard drives and optical discs have limited life spans but as long as the data they contain is regularly copied over to fresh media then problems of degradation can be avoided. This is helped by the fact that digital copies are faithful duplicates of the original artefacts, unlike in the analogue world where excessive copying can result in lower quality backups. A photocopy of a photocopy is an example of the weakness in relying on analogue backups. The main issue for digital archive managers is making sure that the formats in which the data is encoded is one which future generations will be able to make sense of. Many of us still have VCRs in our homes but because we moved to the DVD format for video entertainment over the previous decade, it will become increasingly difficult to play our old video cassettes. As video streaming over the internet becomes more popular through services such as Netflix, our DVDs are likely to go the same way as video cassettes. A digital archive will be of little use if nobody in 100 years has the ability to decode and understand the files it contains.

An example of a digital collection much less than 100 years old that faced this issue is the Domesday Project undertaken by the BBC in 1986 to mark the 900th anniversary of William the Conqueror's land survey of England in the 11th century. The project involved the collation of text and video submissions from schools and members of the public onto video discs to present a snapshot of life in Britain in the mid-1980s. However, only 15 years later it had become almost impossible to find the hardware capable of reading the discs as they were in a format that had not been successful. Can anyone be confident that the JPG format for pictures, the AVI format for video or the PDF format for documents will be readable by our grandchildren in 2030?

This is a question that a number of organizations and research projects are addressing. The Born Digital project funded by the Andrew W. Mellon Foundation and comprising members from the Universities of Hull in the UK and Stanford, Yale and Virginia in the USA is a good example. Started in 2009, the project aims to 'create an inter-institutional framework for stewarding born-digital content' (University of Virginia Library, 2011). As well as devising systems for helping organizations preserve their digital content in accessible formats the project members are looking at ways to ensure that important metadata is not stripped out when digital items are converted from one format to another. It is important to remember that the visible manifestation of such items is not the only facet required for preservation. For example, the metadata associated with digital images and which is seldom seen by those viewing them often includes the time and date the image was taken, the device that took it and, increasingly, where the image was taken through the use of geo tags. Valuable metadata associated with documents can include date of creation, authors, version number as well as indexing terms. As digital collections grow this peripheral information will become increasingly important for information professionals who wish to make sense of their archives.

Keeping it all safe

Information professionals responsible for managing their organization's information know the importance of data security whether to protect against attempts by outsiders to hack into systems or to prevent natural disasters from destroying such resources. At a basic level, processes can be put in place to make sure regular backups are made of important data and that these backup copies are spread across a range of locations. However, sometimes this is not perceived to be sufficient, particularly for organizations that rely on their information resources as their prime source of competitive advantage. Technology and pharmaceutical companies, for example, rely on their research to develop new products and drugs and will make significant investments to ensure their competitors are not aware of their strategic plans. These companies will go to great lengths to lock down sensitive data through restricting internal access and securing it against networked attacks. A recent trend for companies wishing to provide physical security to their data has been to collocate it in secure underground stores, typically ex-nuclear bunkers and abandoned mines. Iron Mountain is a US company that offers such facilities with its main secure premises located in 1.7 million square feet under a mountain in Pennsylvania. One of the advantages of the 200 foot deep mine is that it remains at a constant temperature of 13 degrees centigrade, which negates the need for expensive cooling systems that above-ground data centres require to prevent the computer servers from over-heating. According to Miller (2010) more than 2700 people work in the Iron Mountain facility, which has its own restaurant, water treatment plant, fire engines and backup power systems. Also in the USA, the Mountain Complex is almost twice the size of Iron Mountain and is built into the side of a mountain which, its owners claim, is setting 'the gold standard in secure storage' (www.omuvs.com). Whether such sites really offer the security their clients require is debatable as information security breaches are often down to dishonest or careless employees. However, putting a data centre in a mountain certainly gives the impression of security and gives a new meaning to the term 'data mining'.

Storage at the personal level

Until recently the data that we personally managed typically comprised physical items such as photographs, letters, CDs, DVDs, books and possibly some old school reports and diaries. Spread across shelves and some dusty boxes in the attic, they were easy to manage and followed us as we moved house. Our photographs are now dispersed across memory cards, personal computers, mobile phones and social media sites. Personal correspondence may be in multiple accounts and, like photos, may reside on ours and other people's social media pages. There is a similar story for our music and increasingly books, as e-readers such as the Amazon Kindle and tablet computers become platforms for media consumption. Keeping track of all this information is not easy, particularly when devices such as smartphones, computers and MP3 players are replaced at ever-shortening intervals. Love letters, once treasured and kept for years, are now rather more transient in their digital format and may disappear as soon as you upgrade your computer or switch e-mail provider. Keeping track of all this data and making sure it is backed up and preserved for posterity is forcing many of us to adopt practices that have been the preserve of digital archivists. Table 3.1 presents an overview of some of the media devices commonly found in most households, and their characteristics.

Table 3.1 Personal data storage devices			
Media	Device	Capacity	Format
Music	iPod/MP3 player Smartphone CD player	700MB – 160GB	MP3 AAC WAV CDA Vorbis WMA
Photographs	Digital camera Smartphone Tablet computer	2GB – 64GB	JPEG TIFF RAW
Video	Video camera Smartphone Web cam	2GB – 64GB	H.264 MPEG 1,2,4 MJPEG WMV
Text	PC E-book reader Tablet computer	2GB – 1TB	TXT DOC RTF PDF AZW EPUB

Table 3.1 presents only a summary of some of the core media devices we use in our daily lives and the formats typically used to create and present the data. However, it demonstrates the complexity of competing standards, some open and some proprietary, that we have to consider when working out a preservation plan for it all. It is not unreasonable to assume that a typical

family with children may have produced several thousand gigabytes of digital data over a ten year period. Video would probably make up the bulk of this with an hour of video from a modern consumer camcorder requiring approximately 2 gigabytes of storage. Finding the hardware to store our personal digital archives is probably the easiest part of the problem with 3 terabyte hard drives available in early 2012 for approximately £100. The biggest challenge will be choosing which format to store our data in and then devising and sticking to a plan for regularly backing it all up to secure on-site and off-site locations.

Harris (2009) argues that choosing the right digital format is crucial to avoid creating an archive that will be unreadable in 10 or 20 years' time. For text he recommends using the generic TXT format, which he claims will be readable 100 years from now, and avoid the problems faced by the BBC Domesday Project mentioned earlier. For text documents that also contain images he recommends the PDF format, which is now an ISO standard, but he points out that future changes to the standard by its owner, Adobe, may create compatibility issues in the future. While nobody can be certain which digital formats will be readable in 100 years, it seems likely that the vast numbers of pictures currently held in the JPEG format and music in the MP3 format will ensure some kind of basic decoding software will be available to make sense of them. It is the less commonly used formats, particularly in the more complex area of video encoding, that may cause problems. One can imagine a new type of information professional will be required in the year 2050 who can act as a digital archaeologist and restore inaccessible photos and videos to their owners.

Putting it in the cloud

A fundamental aspect of any data backup plan is to make sure that at least one copy is kept off-site. This has been common practice for most organizations for many years and has led to the rise of facilities such as Iron Mountain discussed earlier. However, there is also a growing trend for private individuals to do the same, with a range of providers offering solutions for backing up personal data on off-site servers. According to Wachter (2010), the market for such services in the USA would be worth $4 billion by 2012. She says that a survey by the consultants Booz and Co. in 2009 showed that consumers were willing to pay $9 a month for a single digital repository for their data. Companies offering off-site backup to consumers include Carbonite, SugarSync, Dropbox and Mozy. Typically these require software to be installed on the devices that need backing up with the backups taking place in the background while the computer is switched on. While they offer an easy way to back up data, there are issues that need to be considered before committing to such services. One is the cost; for relatively small amounts of data some of the companies offer a free service but for anything over several gigabytes a monthly or annual subscription will be required. Dropbox, for example, charges $20 a month (in August 2011) for 100 gigabytes of storage. With most personal computers now having hard drives of over 300 gigabytes it is easy to see how the costs can mount up. Over a ten year period this could add up to thousands of dollars. Another issue is security; how can we be sure that the company we are trusting our data to can be relied on to keep it safe? Stories of computers and networks being hacked are common with even large companies such as Google and Sony vulnerable to determined intruders. Finally, even if our data is secure and locked down, what happens if the company goes out of business? Will our data disappear along with the company or will we be given an opportunity to retrieve it before their servers are switched off? There are no easy answers to these questions but they will be issues many of us will have to deal with. Again, information professionals will be better placed than many to offer advice on this front as they are information management problems that have been faced by organizations for a number of years.

Our digital footprints

Although making sure our digital music, photos and files are preserved safely requires some careful consideration as to formats and storage providers, once those decisions are made it is a relatively simple process of working to a system. Whatever solution is chosen will be based on the notion of backing up and storing discrete files in particular formats. Personal digital curation becomes a little more complicated when we have to deal with less tangible items of information such as e-mails, social media posts and profiles, instant messaging and other digital breadcrumbs we leave behind us as we use the web. Active users of Facebook, for example, will build up considerable archives of posts, photos and other messages shared across their social network, which can present a valuable timeline of their lives. While we can copy our digital photos and music across different devices can we do the same with this other data? If so, how might we do this, in what format might it be, and what other services will be able to make sense of it?

Providing definitive answers to these questions is not possible as social media is still in its infancy and the policies adopted by companies such as Facebook are changing regularly. However, there has been considerable concern over the last several years that users should be able to move their data across different networks and preserve copies for posterity. Google, for example, has set up an engineering team it calls the Data Liberation Front, whose aim is to make it easier for users to move their data in and out of the company's products. The group encourages anyone using a web service that holds their personal data to ask three questions before committing to the service:

1. Can I get my data out in an open, interoperable, portable format?
2. How much is it going to cost to get my data out?
3. How much of my time is it going to take to get my data out?

(www.dataliberation.org)

In an attempt to provide positive answers to the above questions, the Data Liberation Front works with Google's product development teams to make the flow of data as smooth and as easy as possible. As part of this ambition and because of the increasing number of Google services such as Gmail, Google Plus, Picasa, etc., in 2011 the group launched a service called Google Takeout, which allows data to be taken out from multiple Google services in one click. The data is downloaded as a compressed single file, which can then be opened and ported to other compatible services. Facebook offers a similar service for users to download a copy of their data but how easily it can then be uploaded to another social media service is uncertain. It is clearly not in Facebook's commercial interest to make it easy for its users to pack up their data and move to a competitor's site. While a downloaded copy of a Facebook account's data might allow the user to view his or her data offline, it is unlikely that another service would be able to make sense of the complex links with other Facebook users which is at the heart of such a service.

While Google has been at the forefront of delivering so called 'cloud' computing services to consumers, other companies are now also moving in to this space. In 2011 Apple announced the launch of its iCloud service, which will allow users to store their music, video and other digital content in Apple's data centres. According to Harris (2011), the company has spent over $1 billion on a new, 500,000 square foot data centre for its iCloud service. Also in 2011, Amazon started allowing its customers to store music and e-books bought over its service on the company's servers. As well as being an off-site backup service, Amazon's service allows users to access their content anywhere via a web browser. While this may be a convenience for many people it also presents challenges to the traditional ways we have bought and 'owned' content. These challenges are explored in other parts of this book as they impact on information distribution and consumption, but from a storage perspective off-site hosting begins to blur the distinction between owning a piece of content and renting it. When our music was stored on records and

CDs we had legal ownership over that copy and were free to lend or sell it on to others. If our music, books and videos are stored in Amazon's, Google's or Apple's data centres then we may be restricted on how we can legally move that content around. We may be trading ownership for convenience.

So far this section has considered some of the questions we might want to consider when planning a preservation strategy for our personal data. If done correctly it should allow us to look back on our old photos, videos and e-mails in our old age and share them with our grandchildren. However, what happens to that data when we are no longer here? Just as we make wills to allow the transfer of physical and monetary assets when we die should we also be making plans for others to inherit our digital legacy? Carroll and Romano (2010) think so and have written a book, *Your Digital Afterlife*, offering advice for anyone wanting to allow an orderly handover of their digital assets after their death. In the case of digital data stored on traditional media such as computer hard drives and optical discs, such a handover is relatively straightforward and can be managed as part of a traditional will, but with online data it becomes more complicated with issues of passwords and legal questions as to whether social media and e-mail accounts can be transferred. Facebook has attempted to deal with this by creating 'memorialized' profiles for accounts where the owner has died. With over 800 million accounts, including a rapidly growing number of users over the age of 50, this was becoming a growing issue for Facebook. By filling in a form and providing proof that the account holder has died, Facebook will freeze the pages of the deceased, not allow any more logins and prevent the pages from showing up in searches. The comment wall will remain and be a place for friends and family to pay their respects. The pages will then act as a memorial to the deceased user or, if the relatives wish, the pages will be removed completely. It will be interesting to see how the Facebook initiative and developments across other social media platforms develop. Might such companies be legally obliged to maintain memorial sites for minimum periods or in perpetuity as they become valuable sources of the details of our everyday lives for future historians? Perhaps they will begin to take on a similar role to the national archives in terms of preserving our digital heritage.

The future of storage

When it comes to technology, predicting the future is generally a fool's errand but some general directions of travel can be assumed. It now seems inevitable that more of the work that has traditionally been done and then stored on personal computers will be managed by web or cloud services in remote locations. The increasingly pervasive nature of broadband connections, both fixed and mobile, and the popularity of services provided by Facebook, Twitter, Google and Amazon, are accelerating this process. Some of the issues around sustainable formats and security have been discussed above and there is still a lot of work to be done before users can be confident that services are secure and will not lock them in. Organizations are already grappling with these questions and increasingly it will also be a problem for individuals.

One of the defining characteristics of the computing revolution has been a steady increase in the power of devices and a corresponding fall in their cost to users, which, in the context of microprocessors, has been referred to as Moore's law. Data storage is no exception with Smith (2010) calculating that the retail price of computer hard drives fell from approximately $9 per gigabyte in 2000 to 8 cents per gigabyte in 2010, a decrease of 99%. Projecting that decrease forward to 2020 would result in 1 terabyte drives costing less than a dollar. Data storage is being commoditized and its cost will become negligible but it will be the services around storage such as accessibility and security that will command a price premium.

The price example mentioned above uses traditional hard drives comprising spinning magnetic platters to show the fall in prices. However, just as floppy discs are rarely used now, so those types of disc will probably not be in a personal computer bought in 2020. Solid state drives (SSDs) and flash memory cards are the norm in smartphones, tablet computers and most music players and are also appearing in laptops and personal computers. While they are currently more expensive to produce than traditional hard drives, their speed, size, power consumption and lack of moving parts make them attractive for portable device manufacturers. Sales of traditional drives have been falling in recent years and Samsung's sale of its hard drive manufacturing unit in 2011 to Seagate is an indicator that the market is changing to favour new technologies.

One of the biggest challenges for producers of data storage technologies will be to cope with the competing demands for increased storage capacities but at lower prices and with decreased physical footprints and energy consumption but faster access and write speeds. Reducing the energy requirements of data centres is a growing concern for many of the larger internet companies. Much of the energy consumed is used to cool the many thousands of computer servers housed in such centres, which has, according to Fehrenbacher (2011), led Google and Facebook to build centres in Scandinavia to make use of the natural air cooling that the cold winter climate allows. It is a sign that companies are increasingly working with nature to build sustainable businesses rather than consuming ever-increasing amounts of energy to counter the by-products of large-scale computing. As global warming becomes a higher priority for all of us and cloud computing replaces the traditional PC perhaps we will see a migration of computing facilities to the colder northern hemisphere. Radical new techniques for increasing storage capacities are also being explored with holographic discs and even protein-based DVDs under development. Herrman and Buchanan (2010) discuss the possibility of manipulating the DNA of bacteria as a solution, claiming that 'up to 100 bits of data can be attached to each organism. Scientists successfully encoded and attached the phrase "e=mc2 1905" to the DNA of bacillus subtilis, a common soil bacteria.' In the short to medium term we will have to rely on tried and tested storage technologies such as hard drives and SSDs, but the laws of physics may render them obsolete in 10 or 20 years and holograms and bacteria may be the solution to preserving our digital heritage.

Concluding comments

While the amount of information we are creating and storing has never been so large, it has also never been so vulnerable to loss and destruction. Besides the media it is stored on, digital data cannot be seen and the old saying, 'out of sight, out of mind' seems increasingly relevant in this context. Organizations with a legal and commercial interest in preserving data will continue to develop new and innovative ways of doing this but what about the rest of us? When a lifetime's photos, videos and e-mails can be lost as our computer hard drive finally expires, personal information storage solutions will become ever more relevant. Information preservation and collection management policies may no longer be the sole preserve of the information professional.

QUESTIONS TO THINK ABOUT

1. We are still able to marvel at medieval illuminated manuscripts but what will remain of our digital heritage in 1000 years?
2. When every university makes all of its research available through its institutional repository will we still need academic journals?
3. Should public libraries adopt some of the data mining techniques of Walmart and Tesco to better understand their users?
4. What are some of the disadvantages and benefits of storing data in the cloud?

CHAPTER 4
New models of information distribution

Introduction

At the heart of the current information revolution are radical changes to the way information, in all its forms, is distributed. Obviously, the internet has been a key driver of these changes but so too have other advances and investments in communication networks, particularly on the mobile front. By the beginning of 2012 approximately one-third (over 2 billion) of the world's population were connected to the internet while more than three-quarters of the world had a mobile phone. It is across these networks that much of the information we consume is carried. Broadly, we are moving from a centralized broadcast model of information distribution to a more distributed and, some would argue, more democratic model where many of the established information gatekeepers are being bypassed. Just as the railways in the 19th century transformed the movement of goods and people across many western economies, communication systems are doing the same for information. However, a key difference between these networks is the ease of access with which individuals and organizations can access them as well as fundamental differences between the physical world and the digital. Systems for moving objects such as roads and railways are limited in their capacity to carry people and vehicles, as anyone who has to travel in rush hour knows, while digital networks, particularly those using optical fibre, are far less constrained. This chapter explains some of the key technical characteristics of our communication networks within the context of the radical changes that are taking place in the information sector. The competing interests of information producers and network operators are explored and the implications for information professionals considered.

The architecture of the internet

To appreciate the significance of the changes that are taking place in the world of information it is important to understand, at a basic level at least, how the internet works. While anyone who has grown up in the last 15 years, the so called 'digital natives', may take an internet connection for granted it is worth looking back at where this network came from and how it evolved. The significance of this will become clearer when we consider some of the threats to the internet in terms of its open nature and what Zittrain (2008) calls its 'generative' nature. This will be examined at the end of this chapter but first let's look back a few years to when the internet was born.

According to Leiner at al. (2009), the origins of the internet can be traced back to the early 1960s when a researcher at the Massachusetts Institute of Technology (MIT) proposed an idea for what he called a 'Galactic Network' that would comprise a globally distributed set of connected computers. At the same time another MIT researcher published a paper outlining a new method for transporting data across communication networks, called packet switching. The key difference between packet switching and the traditional circuit switching method was that messages were broken down into data packets and could be distributed across a network using multiple connections to be reassembled at the other end into the original message. This was a far more efficient way of moving data and was also more resilient to network faults as packets that did not arrive at the final destination could be sent for again. With a traditional circuit switching method a single connection was required between the sender and the receiver, which slowed down networks, and if a problem occurred then the entire message needed to be sent again. Packet switching allowed networks to carry far more data and at lower cost to those sending and receiving messages. Throughout the 1960s, researchers in the USA and UK explored the potential of packet switching and by 1969 ARPANET, the forerunner of the internet, carried its first message between Stanford University and University of California, Los Angeles. The network was expanded over the 1970s and systems and standards were agreed that allowed services such as e-mail and file transport to be added. These standards or protocols are a key factor in explaining why the internet has evolved to its present state. As Leiner et al. (2009) explain:

> The Internet as we know it embodies a key underlying technical idea, namely that of open architecture networking. In this approach, the choice of any individual network technology was not dictated by a particular network architecture but rather could be selected freely by a provider and made to interwork with the other networks through a meta-level 'Internetworking Architecture'.

Just as any vehicle that is built within certain size parameters can use our road networks, so any computer that complied with freely available protocols could connect to the internet. The internet was developed by researchers who wanted to create a network that would allow the greatest number of people to access it and this was achieved through the creation of and compliance to open standards. The non-profit nature of their endeavours lies at the heart of their creation and is a good example of the role that public bodies can play, albeit often unwittingly, in the development of major innovations.

While the internet continued to grow throughout the 1980s and into the early 1990s it was largely used by the academic community to share information and there was little commercial activity taking place on or around it. Outside universities it was expensive and technically complicated for individuals or organizations to connect to the network with hardware, software and connection charges running into the thousands of dollars. At this time other private networks started to emerge that offered users access to a range of information and communication services. These included Compuserve, Delphi and America Online (AOL) and were designed to offer a limited range of proprietary and sometimes third party information services such as news, discussion forums and early versions of electronic mail. One of the limitations of such networks was their 'walled garden' approach to service provision where subscribers were limited to offerings vetted by the provider. From a commercial perspective this control has a certain logic; why go to the expense of building a network via which anyone can deliver services that could compete with the network owner's offerings? Controlling what is offered over the network allows the owner to take a greater share of the revenues that flow over the network. The downside for users to such an arrangement is a restriction of choice and stifling of innovation as well as limitations as to what can be done on the network. Sending e-mails between CompuServe subscribers was fine but the problems arose when you wanted to send an e-mail to someone on another network as they were not designed to be interoperable. Similar networks were experimented with by some of the large cable television (CATV) operators at this time where the notion of interactive television looked like becoming a reality. CATV networks, unlike traditional terrestrial television broadcast networks, had wires going into subscribers' homes, which could be used for both sending information down to households and receiving an upstream from them. A two-way stream could allow customers to request information services such as the delivery of videos on demand (VOD) and online banking as well as the delivery of physical items such as pizzas and groceries. One of the largest interactive television trials took place in Orlando, Florida, in the mid-1990s where Time Warner invested over $100 million in providing set top boxes and upgraded network connections to thousands of subscribers. However, the high infrastructure costs and the lack of enthusiasm amongst subscribers for the more expensive services offered led to its cancellation in 1997.

One of the fundamental issues that users of online networks such as CompuServe and interactive CATV networks such as Time Warner's faced was lack of choice. The services they offered were dictated by the network owners so pizzas could only be ordered from one company that had tied up an exclusive deal with Time Warner or news was provided by a CompuServe-approved supplier. This bore little resemblance to the high street or the shopping mall where competing shops and banks are free to ply their wares and customers can choose based on price, quality and level of service provision. Ultimately, this is one of the key reasons for the failure of such networks to survive once the internet began to open up to end-users outside universities. It was the development in the 1990s of the world wide web as a graphical interface, sitting on top of the internet as an open distribution network, that provided users and information service providers with the incentive they needed to move to this 'new' environment, which had quietly been growing since the 1970s. Isenberg (1998) refers to the internet as the 'stupid network' in ironic reference to the so called 'intelligent networks' that were being promoted by the major telecommunication networks. The ability of these operators to offer services such as caller ID and call transfer relied on centralized computer switching within the network and relatively simple telephone devices at the consumer end. Isenberg's 'stupid network' was only concerned with moving digital bits from sender to receiver and left it up to the computing devices at either end to make sense of them. This new model of information distribution threatened the control that network operators had traditionally exercised and put the users in a position of power for the first time.

By the mid-1990s it was becoming clear to many that the 'open' internet had a more promising future than the closed networks described above, as it allowed anyone who was using the right equipment to connect with each other. E-mail took on a new lease of life as it was no longer controlled by commercially motivated organizations and became the internet's first 'killer application'. The world wide web then allowed more than just text-based information to be presented to users, with a website becoming as indispensable to organizations as having a telephone or fax number. The launch of the Mosaic web browser in 1993 along with the rise of e-mail as a communications tool brought the internet into the mainstream, and by 1995 there were an estimated 16 million users worldwide. Within three years this had grown to almost 150 million and by the end of 2000 there were 360 million global users. At the same time the cost to users of connecting to the internet fell as did the computing hardware, but connection speeds increased. In 1995 the typical domestic download speed was 14.4 kilobits per second (kbs), which restricted the types of data that could be downloaded to text and low resolution graphics. Gradually the speed of modems increased but it was not until the introduction of broadband connections either using the ADSL technologies of the telephone companies or high speed CATV connections that higher bandwidth services such as telephony or video streaming were possible.

When it became clear that the internet was more than a fad like CB Radio had been in the 1970s, the financial community began to take an interest and by the late 1990s the first internet boom had begun. Telecom operators invested millions in upgrading their networks and laying fibre optic cables across most of the developed world. New entrants such as Global Crossing and Level 3 Communications raised hundreds of millions of dollars on the capital markets to build out entirely new fibre networks in anticipation of the rapidly growing demand for bandwidth. It resembled the building of the railway networks in the UK and USA in the mid-19th century when speculators raised money from investors to fund what they saw as the future of transportation. Unfortunately for many of these investors the result was the same: the networks were built but the financial returns were not as expected and fortunes were lost. Global Crossing, for example, had built a high speed data network spanning 27 countries by 2002 but as bandwidth prices fell due to over-capacity the company declared bankruptcy in that year with debts of over $12 billion. However, as with the railways, what was bad news for investors was ultimately good news for internet users as the legacy of companies like Global Crossing was a backbone network fit for the 21st century. The dotcom bust of 2000 may have cleared out a number of weak companies built on flimsy business models but it paved the way for the second generation of internet companies commonly referred to as Web 2.0.

Distribution and disintermediation

We've seen how the internet has developed from humble beginnings in university research centres and how it has emerged as a key network for distributing information. This section considers the impact it is having on a range of information-intensive industries and the information professionals that rely on the internet as a distribution network. In Chapter 2 we saw how new technologies are leading to the creation of new types of information and in this chapter we will explore how those technologies are changing the way information is carried from creators to end-users and, in many instances, leading to the disintermediation of traditional gatekeepers, including information professionals. Disintermediation refers to the bypassing of established players in a value chain either through the introduction of new technologies or via new business processes. In the physical world the growth of farm shops can be seen as an attempt by farmers to disintermediate wholesale and retailers and sell their produce directly to consumers. Although this has not checked the growth of large supermarkets, such ventures along with farmers' markets allow the original producers of our food to keep a larger share of the profits. In Chapter 2 we saw how bloggers were attempting to do something similar in their attempts to bypass traditional publishing models. If you are a producer of information then the internet presents an obvious channel to get your content directly to your customers without having to go through intermediaries, which would want to take their share of profits out of the value chain. However, the theoretical prospects for information distribution promised by the internet do not always work in practice. In a number of instances we are seeing new intermediaries such as Amazon, iTunes and eBay dislodging established players from the physical world but still acting as gatekeepers between buyers and sellers.

In the information world the internet has been a disruptive force for both providers of information services as well as the information professionals who buy them. Perhaps the most obvious impact has been on the information that has relied on paper as its distribution method, with directories and encyclopaedias suffering the most. However, it should be remembered that digital online information services predate the world wide web by almost 20 years. In 1972 the Lockheed Corporation offered online access to its Dialog set of databases for a fee, starting an industry of commercial online information access that continues into the 21st century. Owners of databases and information products realized there was a potential to sell their assets through hosts such as Dialog, DataStar and Orbit to interested parties. Purchasers tended to be librarians and information professionals who were often the only people trained to interrogate such databases. Proper training was important as the hosts were difficult to search, with each having their own search languages and syntax. The databases were also expensive to access, typically charging a usage fee depending on the time spent on the service and the amount of data downloaded. The data access fees charged by the local telecommunications operator and the modem and terminal hardware also added to the cost. These financial and technical barriers restricted who could access the service as inefficient searching could result in substantial costs to the person requiring the information. According to Williams (2005), there were 4018 online databases on offer by 1990, with the vast majority only accessible through hosts such as Dialog. Several thousand databases were also accessible via other media such as CD-ROM, diskette and magnetic tape but throughout the 1990s these declined in significance as online access became the norm. By 2004 the number of online databases had grown to 9489 but Williams (2005) points out that by then their growth had slowed.

Two of the key changes for database providers that have taken place since the late 1990s are a move to using the internet as their platform for delivery and the web as the interface for users to search for information. While some of the large database hosts still allow users to search using their proprietary command languages they have also introduced simplified searching making the experience closer to an internet search engine. They have also experimented with different charging methods in an attempt to encourage more casual searchers to try their services. However, this has been met with mixed and often disappointing responses as many information seekers do not expect to pay for information accessed over the internet and will often be satisfied with free sources. The struggles by large information vendors such as Thomson, Dow Jones and Reuters to adapt to this new world of 'free' information can be seen in the corporate mergers and joint ventures that have taken place over the previous 15 years but which have yet to find a business model that will attract non-information professionals to pay for information. At the core of this problem for vendors is the much used and often misunderstood phrase, 'Information wants to be free'. The phrase is attributed to Stewart Brand who, according to Clarke (2000), said at a hacker conference in 1984:

> On the one hand information wants to be expensive, because it's so valuable. The right information in the right place just changes your life. On the other hand, information wants to be free, because the cost of getting it out is getting lower and lower all the time. So you have these two fighting against each other.

CASE STUDY – STOCKTWITS

Some of the largest and most profitable areas of online information services are those used by financial services companies. Organizations such as Bloomberg and Thomson Reuters provide real-time data services for financial market traders in a market for such data worth over $40 billion. While investment banks still rely primarily on the large, established information providers, there is a growing trend of smaller companies entering the market and making use of the internet and social media platforms to deliver their services. StockTwits was established in 2009 and makes use of Twitter to track what people are saying about specific stocks on the network. StockTwits users can follow particular analysts and commentators whom they trust and make investment decisions based on what is being said. The basic StockTwits service is free with a premium service costing $99 a month. While many would argue that Twitter is not a likely source of valuable information on which to base investment decisions, the half a million monthly visitors to the site might have a different view. Whether social media services offer viable platforms on which to build a profitable information business remains to be seen but companies like StockTwits demonstrate the disruptive power of the internet as an information distribution network.

The internet is now a highly efficient distribution network for exchanging information and is forcing information providers to re-evaluate their business models (see case study above). When information was scarce and difficult to access it was possible to charge a premium for it but when information that is perceived to be 'good enough' is easily available at no cost then the equation changes. This is also having an impact on information professionals, who have traditionally been the gatekeepers to online databases. The advent of desktop computers, the internet and then search engines such as Google has, for many people, bypassed the need to go to a librarian.

The new intermediaries

It is the intrinsic nature of information and, in particular, the characteristics of digital information, that gives credence to the notion that information may want to be free. Shapiro and Varian (1999) explain the concept of 'first-copy costs' whereby the cost of an information product such as a book or a film is sunk into the cost of producing the first copy. Once that first book is published then the subsequent copies comprise only the marginal cost of printing. Their seminal work on the internet and its impact on information producers leads them to comment:

> Information delivered over a network in digital form exhibits the first-copy problem in an extreme way: once the first copy of the information has been produced, additional copies cost essentially nothing.
>
> (Shapiro and Varian, 1999)

Combining these characteristics with the non-rivalrous nature of digital information presents challenges to anyone hoping to make money from its sale. Non-rivalry is an economic term referring to commodities such as information whose consumption by one person does not prohibit their consumption by another. A newspaper, for example, is not destroyed by being read whereas a cake can only be eaten once. Digital information suffers even less from rivalry in that multiple digital copies can be read at once whereas an analogue equivalent such as a book can only be read by one person at a time.

Intermediaries in the shadows

One of the sectors that has been impacted the most by the rise of the internet has been the music industry. The popularity of the CD format for music throughout the 1980s and 1990s meant that when the internet started to become popular amongst consumers, most young people already had digital collections of music that could relatively easily be ripped from CDs to computer hard drives. The MP3 compression format for audio files made it possible for large music collections to be shrunk to one-tenth their size in terms of the storage space they required. Smaller file sizes were also easier to send over the internet, an important factor when most people still relied on slow dial-up connections. These developments conspired in the late 1990s to create an environment where a 19-year-old university student called Shawn Fanning created and launched an internet-based music sharing system called Napster, which within a year had amassed 20 million users who were sharing 80 million songs. In terms of creating a vibrant and popular service, Napster was a great success but its disregard for US copyright law brought it to the attention of the music industry and in 2001, after a series of legal battles in the courts, the service was shut down. In some ways the Napster story remains a footnote in the history of the internet as the company lasted little more than a year and never managed to develop a profitable and, more importantly, legal business model. However, the story also highlights the disruptive nature of the internet as a distribution system for digital information and the threat it poses to established industries. Knopper (2009) quotes Kearby, founder of an online music service, describing his experience of dealing with music industry executives in the late 1990s:

> Some of them were more interested in experimenting than others, there's no doubt about it. But they were, in effect, buggy-whip manufacturers, trying to keep the auto at bay as long as they could.   (Knopper, 2009)

Napster was followed by similar initiatives such as LimeWire and Kazaa, which made use of peer-to-peer technologies to allow users to share sections of their computer hard drives primarily for the purpose of sharing music but also increasingly for video files. Video compression protocols were allowing movies to be compressed into smaller files in the same way that the MP3 format had done for music. LimeWire and Kazaa met with similar legal objections from the music industry as Napster and they were eventually forced to prevent their users from trading copyright-infringing materials. More recently, The Pirate Bay has been the centre of attention from the music and film industries and by mid-2011 claimed to have over 5 million registered users as well as being in the top 100 of most visited websites globally. Despite legal efforts to shut the service down, the Swedish-based operation continues to provide a central place to search for bittorrent files. Bittorrent technology is an efficient way of distributing digital files across the internet using peer-to-peer principles. It works most effectively for popular files, as separate sections of a file are downloaded simultaneously from multiple computers on the peer-to-peer network. This reduces the bandwidth strain on any individual computer's network connection and spreads the load across the internet. The popularity of bittorrent sites such as The Pirate Bay, Torrentz and IsoHunt amongst file shares can be seen by examining internet traffic, with bittorrent traffic accounting for over 50% of upstream data flows from users' computers and approximately 20% of downloads across Europe and the USA in early 2011 (Sandvine, 2011). Envisional, a company specializing in monitoring internet activity, estimates that in 2010, 24% of all internet traffic was made up of copyright-infringing data with the majority of this coming from bittorrent files (Envisional, 2011). Combining this figure with internet switch manufacturer Cisco's estimate that global internet traffic in 2010 was approximately 180,000 petabytes, we might assume the volume of illegal files being transported across the internet in 2010 was 43,000 petabytes, the equivalent of almost 11 billion DVDs (Cisco, 2011). If an average value of £5 was given to each of those notional DVDs then a total value of approximately £55 billion could be ascribed to global piracy over the internet in 2010. These figures need to be treated carefully as they are based on traffic samples and average values but they provide some clues as to why music and film business executives have been concerned about file sharing networks over the previous decade. As soon as one network is shut down or blocked by internet service providers another seems to emerge offering users even faster ways to download files and evade copyright law enforcers. Certainly sales of CDs and, more recently, DVDs have been falling since 2000, with a 20% drop in CD sales in 2010 alone, according to Davoudi (2011). However, the extent to which this is due to online piracy or a growing preference amongst consumers for downloaded content is debatable. The following section considers legitimate attempts to use the internet as a distribution tool which, although favoured by many in the music industry, are still bypassing traditional intermediaries such as retail and rental stores.

Copyright-friendly intermediaries

The launch of the iTunes online music store in 2003 marked the beginning of a serious fight back by the music industry to sell music over the internet. Created by Apple Computer, Inc. as a way to allow its iPod customers to buy music online, the initiative has been a rare success and in early 2010 announced its 10 billionth song download. Competitors have emerged since 2003 but, with the exception of Amazon's music download service launched in 2008, none have come close to replicating the success of iTunes. Music streaming services such as Pandora, Last.fm and Spotify have also gained in popularity and possibly present a transition away from buying and 'owning' music to a rental model. This is more akin to the broadcast model we are familiar with, such as radio and television, but offers consumers the advantage of more choice as to what is played. However, the impact on intermediaries in the value chain such as shops is the same. The impact on the content creators, the musicians, may also be considerable. While streaming services, particularly those such as Pandora that offer recommendations, may help emerging artists break through to the mainstream there are financial implications as well. According to McCandless (2010), for musicians to earn the US monthly minimum wage of $1160, they would need to sell 143 self-pressed CDs at $9.99 a unit, 1161 CDs via a music retailer, 1229 album downloads via iTunes or just over 4 million plays on Spotify. McCandless acknowledges that these figures are based on assumptions about the royalty deal a musician will have made with a record company but they illustrate the difficulties of making money in this new environment. However, once a new technology becomes favoured by consumers it is virtually impossible to persuade those consumers to revert back to an old one. Manufacturers of VCR players, audio cassettes and transistor radios will testify to that. We are now seeing similar developments in the book publishing industry as sales of e-book readers, particularly the Amazon Kindle, took off in 2011 alongside the demise of many bookshops, including more than 500 operated by Borders, which went into liquidation in the same year.

Online video – we're all celebrities now

We've seen how the music industry is being turned upside down by the internet as an alternative distribution network for its content. Something similar is also occurring in the distribution of video content as Hollywood and the television broadcast companies struggle to cope with viewers seeking their entertainment from alternative providers such as YouTube and BitTorrent. Whereas in the past you needed complex distribution agreements with cinema or broadcast network owners for your films and programmes to be seen by a mass audience, there is a ready audience of over 2 billion internet users freely accessible to view your masterpiece. YouTube celebrities such as Justin Bieber and Rebecca Black have used this free video network to attract millions of fans and secure lucrative contracts with more mainstream media companies. Amateur musician Rebecca Black's Friday music video was viewed almost 170 million times in its first three months on YouTube in 2011, while the popularity of Justin Bieber's home-made pop videos brought him to the attention of the music industry. While these high-profile examples are exceptions, with most amateur videos never receiving more than a few hundred viewings, it is the scale of YouTube as a video distribution network that is most worthy of attention. Founded in 2005 by three young entrepreneurs, it was bought 18 months later by Google for $1.65 billion and since then has become the dominant online space for posting and viewing video. By May 2011 over 48 hours of video were being uploaded to the service every minute with 3 billion viewings of its videos every day (SearchEngineWatch, 2011). One of the key reasons for its success is the ease with which videos can be uploaded at no cost to the uploader or viewer. However, another important factor is how YouTube makes it easy for people to share videos across the internet by allowing videos to be embedded within other websites. Rather than expecting everyone to visit the YouTube website to view video content, the company offers a unique embed code that can be pasted into other sites. While this may reduce the number of visitors to its own site, it capitalizes on the viral nature of some internet content by encouraging its propagation across other websites.

In this way YouTube is making the most of two features of the internet that distinguishes it from traditional broadcast media networks. Firstly, it is building its service on an open distribution network that treats video data streams the same as any other internet traffic and allows anyone with an internet connection to upload and view video content. Secondly, it is leveraging open web standards to allow video content to be freely shared across other people's and companies' websites, a bold point of difference from most media organizations, which seek to control how their content is consumed. While most people still view video content through their television there are signs that YouTube is moving into becoming more of a distribution service for mainstream content. In 2009 over 10 million people watched a live streamed U2 concert via YouTube, marking a significant move into competing directly with broadcast media networks. In late 2011 the company announced it would be offering UK internet users the opportunity to pay for 30 day rentals of major movies following a similar move in the USA and Canada.

The longer term impact that the internet and YouTube in particular will have on established distribution networks for video content will take a number of years to become apparent. However, on a smaller scale many organizations are making use of the service to offer educational video content to end-users. Universities are increasingly uploading videos of lectures, allowing anyone anywhere in the world to view world-leading academics talk about their specialist subject areas. In the USA, the Massachusetts Institute of Technology (MIT) has been an active user of YouTube since 2005 and by late 2011 had uploaded almost 1800 videos, which had received over 30 million views, with its dedicated channel having more than 118,000 subscribers. The videos that MIT uploads are primarily recordings of formal lectures, opening up one of the world's leading universities to a global audience. While these recordings will never attract the audience numbers that Justin Bieber and Rebecca Black enjoy, it might reasonably be argued that their impact on learning and development will be significantly higher.

Even more ambitious in its attempt to open up learning to those wishing to improve their education is the Khan Academy, discussed in the case study below. The common link between the Khan Academy and those universities uploading their lectures to YouTube and other online platforms is a belief that education does not need to be restricted to the classroom and lecture theatre. The internet presents a supplementary and possibly even, some would argue, an alternative to mainstream education. Apple Computer's iTunes U is an embodiment of this as it brings together its iTunes online library as a distribution service with the educational content of many of the world's leading universities. While iTunes U is perhaps less open than the open web as a platform for distribution, as it requires the use of iTunes software and devices such as the iPod which can run the software, it is an important development in the spread of online learning. Once the appropriate software and hardware are in place it is free to use and allows users to download more than 350,000 lectures, audio and video, from more than 800 universities including Oxford University and The Open University in the UK and Stanford and Yale universities in the USA. In many cases the multimedia content is supplemented by PDF and EPUB format materials.

However, it is important to remember that a university education involves more than simply attending lectures, making notes and sitting exams. Much of the learning takes place in the seminars and tutorials where concepts are discussed and students are encouraged to explore ideas, explain opposing arguments and develop the crucial skill of critical thinking. Writing about the power of technology to transform established industries and organizational practices, Jarvis (2009) acknowledges the limitations of online learning and explains that while it may be useful to develop a specific skill, such as how to learn video editing or speak French, it can never replace a good teacher for more complex endeavours such as understanding the principles of thermodynamics, the philosophy of science or heart surgery. However, Jarvis does believe services like iTunes and YouTube have the potential to alter the way universities will work in the future. He argues that:

> Universities need to ask what value they add in educational transactions. We
> need to ask when and why it is necessary to be in the same room with fellow

students and instructors. Classroom time is valuable but not always necessary.

(Jarvis, 2009)

So perhaps when education is freed from the classroom and, where appropriate, makes use of new distribution platforms, the way we think about schools and universities will change. Moving from an age of scarcity where class sizes were limited by physical spaces to one where a lecture can be seen by millions of people and reviewed as many times as required by those struggling to understand difficult concepts will require different thinking on the part of those managing our educational establishments. For some this will be disruptive as it will require new ways of working and learning but, as businesses are finding across many sectors, when information finds new ways of flowing to those who need it there is little that can be done to stop it.

CASE STUDY – THE KHAN ACADEMY

Established in 2006 by Salman Khan, the Khan Academy operates as a not-for-profit educational organization, which offers free access to over 2500 video lectures and tutorials, primarily on scientific and technical subjects. Salman Khan started the Academy after receiving positive feedback from viewers of short videos he had posted to YouTube to help his cousin with his mathematics homework. Since then he has received funding from Google and the Bill and Melinda Gates Foundation, which has enabled the tutorials to become more sophisticated with users able to complete interactive lessons at their own pace. Users are able to access the service at home, and teachers can integrate Khan Academy lessons into their teaching and monitor the progress of students as they work through the online lessons. The Khan Academy YouTube channel had by late 2011 received over 90 million views and had almost 200,000 subscribers. While online educational resources have been in use since the beginning of the web, what makes this initiative unique is the volume of materials it contains, its interactive features that work with classroom teaching and, perhaps most important, that it is free. The Khan Academy's mission is to 'provide a world-class education to anyone, anywhere' (www.khanacademy.org). In a similar way to the iTunes U initiative, it is taking advantage of an open and easy to access network to overcome the traditional model of education delivery based on the principles of scarcity.

Internet entrepreneur Jeff Dachis's comment in the 1990s that 'everything that can be digital, will be' (Dishman, 2011) seems increasingly prescient and one that information professionals cannot ignore as they plan their careers over the coming decade. Many creators of information, whether for educational, business or entertainment purposes, have seen their value chains disrupted and, in many cases, made less profitable. Intermediaries further down the chain have also suffered as the new distribution networks for digital content have bypassed them entirely. The following section explores the impact these changes are having on the public sector and, in particular, how our governments communicate with us.

Open government and the internet

The notion of open government refers to the perceived right of citizens to have access to information about the workings of government and the decisions that are made in the process of governance at local and national levels. Increasingly, the principles of open government are becoming enshrined in legislation, such as freedom of information laws, which places obligations on public sector bodies to release certain types of information when requested. While some countries such as the UK, Japan and Germany have only enacted such legislation since 2000, others have been more progressive, with Sweden adopting aspects of open government in its constitution in the late 18th century. The principles of open government lie at the heart of any democracy with the belief that for citizens to make informed decisions about who should govern them, free access to relevant information about issues of state is required. It is hard to hold politicians and civil servants to account at the ballot box for their actions if we do not know what they have been doing while in office. There are obvious exceptions to this accountability when it comes to issues of national security and law enforcement

Proactive government

Legislation relating to freedom of information and the obligations such laws put on public bodies is a natural focus for anyone interested in open government. However, information technologies, in particular the internet, have probably had a similar impact in terms of opening up the workings of government. Traditionally, information from government and public bodies has been mediated by journalists, whether through the work of investigative assignments, party political broadcasts or interviews. The media still plays an important role in holding politicians and public servants to account but the internet has provided a direct channel through which public bodies can communicate with citizens. This was possible in the pre-internet era through the use of government advertising campaigns on public interest matters such as health, safe driving and crime issues where billboards, newspaper advertisements and leaflets would be deployed to get messages across. While these techniques are still used, they are expensive and not always effective in reaching the people who want or need the information. Dissemination via websites is becoming increasingly important as a method for making public information easily available. Research in the UK by the Central Office of Information (COI, 2010) underlines this and shows that the 46 websites managed by British central government departments attracted 568 million visitors between April 2009 and March 2010, generating 2.5 billion page impressions. However, despite the efficiency of the internet as a distribution network, maintaining those 46 sites required significant investment with £128 million spent over the year on staff and other costs. A survey of users of 17 of the sites was carried out to determine their satisfaction levels with an average of 30% stating they had found all or most of what they were looking for. It is debatable whether this figure should be higher, with the amount of money being spent on maintaining the websites but it could be argued that, given the high number of visitors and pages that were looked at, it presents reasonable value for money. Certainly the cost of pushing out that volume of information using traditional methods such as advertising and leaflets would be considerably higher. The benefits of more proactive public websites were recognized in 1998 when the UK-based Campaign for Freedom of Information (CFoI) presented an award to the BSE Inquiry for its website. The BSE Inquiry had been set up in 1998 to investigate the spread among cattle of the disease bovine spongiform encephalopathy (BSE), commonly called mad cow disease, and its spread to humans. The inquiry took place in an atmosphere of mistrust among the British public who felt they had been misled by the Government as to the dangers posed by eating meat from infected cattle. The Campaign for the Freedom of Information applauded the openness of the inquiry and the documentation it made available via its website. Evidence for witness statements was uploaded to the site within hours of it being taken, allowing interested parties to see at first hand what was being said rather than relying solely on media reporting or printed transcripts that were normally charged for. According to the CFoI (1998), in the first six weeks of the inquiry, some 7500 witness statements had been downloaded and 14,000 copies of transcripts had been downloaded by visitors from 64 countries.

Defensive government

Across most developed countries the internet has been used by public bodies to make information more accessible to citizens and, most would argue, that was a positive development in strengthening the democratic process. However, the proactive pushing of information out by government through its own websites can be contrasted with the publishing of information by third parties, which may not be so welcome by those in power. One of the key functions of journalists has been to expose wrongdoing by those in power but the internet is allowing others to join in this process. The WikiLeaks website is a good example of how the internet can circumvent traditional communication channels in a similar way that Napster did with the music industry. Set up in 2006 and fronted by Julian Assange, the WikiLeaks site claims to be:

> a non-profit media organization dedicated to bringing important news and information to the public. We provide an innovative, secure and anonymous way for independent sources around the world to leak information to our journalists. We publish material of ethical, political and historical significance while keeping the identity of our sources anonymous, thus providing a universal way for the revealing of suppressed and censored injustices.
>
> (www.wikileaks.org)

In terms of leaking information to journalists, the organization has certainly been a success and been at the centre of a number of high-profile stories relating to the Iraq war, prisoner detentions in Guantanamo Bay, confidential diplomatic cables and others. In many respects the site is simply carrying on a long tradition of helping the media publish stories based on leaked, confidential information. However, it is the scale of the operation and the open publishing of the leaked information on its website that has caught the attention of governments, security services and the media. The site offers links to millions of downloadable files with hundreds of thousands relating to the Iraq war alone that had been classified as confidential by the US military. Despite attempts, some temporarily successful, by public bodies around the world to shut the WikiLeaks site down, it has managed to maintain a web presence. In part this is due to the determination of its backers, but also to the nature of the internet itself, with the hosting of the site moving between and across countries making it less vulnerable to legal or technical attempts to close it down. Whether WikiLeaks will survive in the longer term remains to be seen but it seems unlikely that, under the current structure and governance of the internet, we will return to the more restricted information distribution model that existed before 2006. The constant demand by both the media and much of the general public for greater openness by public bodies and the growth in technologies that facilitate this will ensure that governments will find it harder, if not impossible, to turn back the clock.

Helping the information flow both ways

Most research on open government has concentrated on how public bodies can, either through choice or by statute, make access to information easier and, as we have seen, the internet has played a part in this. However, more recently interest has also been shown in how citizens and organizations outside government can use technology to feed information into public bodies. The growth of Web 2.0 and social media services has encouraged this development as more internet users expect to be able to interact online rather than simply be recipients in a one-way flow of information. In the UK in 2009 the COI produced a guide (COI, 2009) for civil servants on how best to engage with citizens using social media, which made the claim that proper use of social media such as blogs, Facebook and Twitter could improve public engagement with government activities and save money in the process. Gibson (2010) believes that local government can make good use of social media to improve service delivery and argues that:

> . . . not engaging now represents a far greater risk than engaging. Citizens will still use these networks to talk about you, whether you add your voice to the conversation or not. . . . The challenge for all councils now is to move social media off their list of challenges, and on to their list of opportunities.
>
> (Gibson, 2010)

Gibson's observation that social media users will talk about public bodies online whether or not those organizations choose to take part is now becoming a fact of life for both the public and private sectors. When an issue, local or national, captures the public imagination there is now a variety of online places for the matter to be discussed, often to the detriment of those directly involved. De Saulles (2011) measured the involvement with social media of 55 English local government authorities by investigating how they were engaging with Twitter, Facebook, YouTube and Flickr. The results of the survey conducted in late 2010 showed a wide range of engagement by the bodies with only one using all four services and 17 not using any of them to communicate with their electors. However, the same survey repeated eight months later revealed only six authorities still not engaging with any of the social media sites and a significant proportion of the others ramping up their activities.

For many public servants, as well as employees in the private sector, engaging with others across social media is a challenge. Posting information to websites and letting users take it or leave it is one thing but soliciting feedback and taking part in online conversations is quite another. The COI guide is a response to this issue but it goes deeper than simply asking individuals to comment on aspects of government activity. The natural extension of these initiatives is to develop a far more responsive public sector that reconfigures many of its back-office functions and processes to adapt to an interactive digital world. This would be a move beyond services such as allowing users to renew parking permits online to allowing citizens more direct involvement in policy making and driving the agenda of government. Initiatives such as e-petitions, set up by the British Government, indicate where this may be going. The idea behind e-petitions is simple: any British citizen or resident can create a petition using the website and if it achieves more than 100,000 online signatures from other British citizens within a year the subject in question may be debated in Parliament. Launched in July 2011, it will be interesting to see how actively the British public engages with the service and, just as importantly, how responsive the Government is to the petitions it receives. An indicator of how certain issues can generate substantial interest is that within a week of a petition being created asking for benefits to be withdrawn from anyone found guilty of taking part in the riots and looting in England in 2011, over 250,000 signatures had been received. Just as social media sites such as Facebook had been used by some to encourage rioting and looting, the same technologies were also being deployed to give a voice to the quieter, but clearly angry, majority.

Making money from public information

The information industry has long relied on the public sector as a key primary source for many of the products and services that are sold to end-users. Company financial data, for example, originates in most countries from legal obligations placed on private enterprises to submit their annual and sometimes quarterly accounts to public bodies such as Companies House in the UK and, for publicly quoted companies, the Securities and Exchange Commission (SEC) in the USA. Weather data, property and land registrations, census information, data on industrial outputs and a raft of other information are a result of publicly funded operations. Putting a value on these activities is difficult as much of the information is given away or never leaves the organizations that collected it in the first place. Cross (2007) cites estimates which claim that the value of Ordnance Survey mapping data was worth £79 billion to the British economy in 2006 because of the range of industries that relied on it. Some have claimed this figure to be too high but even halving it leaves a very large sum and extrapolating it across other government departments indicates the importance of public sector information (PSI) to the national economies.

A key debate amongst those concerned with PSI centres is the extent to which public bodies should seek to maximize their financial returns by selling their information assets. On the surface it seems logical that the cash-strapped public sector should do all it can to achieve value for money for tax payers and if money can be raised from information buyers in the private sector then that course should be pursued. However, there are also strong arguments made that the public interest is better served in the longer term by PSI being given away to interested parties who should then be free to turn it into commercial products and services. The rationale behind this argument is that more economic activity in terms of job creation and tax receipts will be generated from a vibrant private market in developing information products than from short-term financial gains to public bodies through selling information. Evidence from European research carried out by consultants PIRA (2000) for the European Union would support the case for freeing up information exchange based on comparisons between European and US federal bodies. In the USA there has long been a tradition that information produced via the activities of the federal government should be freely available for third parties to use for commercial purposes. As a consequence a thriving market has developed that repackages financial, weather and mapping data to create paid-for information products. Figure 4.1 presents a

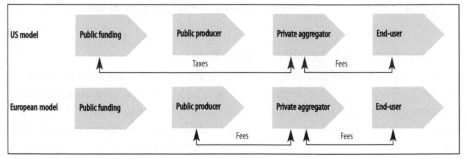

Figure 4.1 Models of public sector information reuse

simplified comparison of the USA and European PSI models and shows the flows of money between the key stakeholders. The PIRA (2000) research estimated that in Europe, where government agencies typically charged for the data they produced, there was an average net financial return to the national economy of seven times the initial investment made by the agency in producing the data. However, in the USA where no charges were made for the data there was a net return of 39 times the initial investment. While this may seem a compelling reason for opening up the markets for PSI there are also counter arguments that suggest agencies which are allowed to make a financial return on their information outputs are more likely to reinvest those profits into producing higher quality data sets. Agencies that rely solely on public funding for their operations, it is argued, will not have the resources to maintain such standards. In Europe the pressure for change resulted in a European Directive in 2003 on the reuse of public sector information and this had been enacted into national laws by all EU members by 2008. Critics of the Directive point out that, although its intention was to create a more vibrant PSI market along the lines of the US model, its wording has allowed member states to avoid fully opening up their markets. The UK has been one of the more progressive EU members in terms of applying the Directive and in 2005 incorporated it into national law. Responsibility for ensuring that public bodies comply with the law rests with The National Archives, which has taken a proactive role in helping organizations adapt their information management practices to this new environment of greater data sharing.

Advocates of greater data sharing by public bodies in the UK were given a boost in 2010 when the incoming Conservative/Liberal Democrat Coalition Government created a Transparency Board whose responsibilities included 'establishing public data principles across the public sector and making datasets available for potential development and re-use' (The National Archives, 2011). This was followed up in late 2011 when £10 million of public funding was put into supporting the Open Data Institute, a body set up to support UK companies that wish to reuse public information. Data will come from a range of bodies including weather data from the Met Office and house price data from the Land Registry. Although, in the shorter term, some of these bodies may suffer a loss of income from the commercial sale of data, in the longer term there may be broader benefits for the British economy and society. According to Hall (2011), 'the potential for the injection of up to £16 billion into the flagging UK economy could be too powerful a stimulus to ignore'. It is significant that the Open Data Institute is based in Shoreditch in East London, an area well known for its concentration of innovative, internet companies. Perhaps this signifies a belated but welcome recognition by government that information rather than just technology is at the heart of many of the innovative web services that are stimulating economic growth.

For the information profession these developments present an opportunity to take a more central role in public sector information management. While more traditional library-based roles may be cut back across many national and local bodies, the demand for information professionals with the skills to manage and manipulate data to comply with the new agenda for greater sharing is growing. These skills include an understanding of open standards for data management and how to allow sharing through application programming interfaces (APIs), breaking down the information silos that many public bodies have built up and which make sharing difficult. Developing these skills will require changes from employers in terms of the training they offer their information professionals and librarians as well as a reconfiguration of many of the LIS courses which prepare graduates for information work.

Threats to the open web

At the beginning of this chapter the writer Jonathan Zittrain was mentioned in the context of his notion of the 'generative' nature of the internet. In his book, *The Future of the Internet*, Zittrain (2008) explains why the internet has been such an important source of innovation over the last 20 years and why changes to the way the internet is managed and used may stifle future innovations. He points out that the network can be thought of as a series of layers, with the physical layer of wires, cables and routers at the bottom, overlaid by the protocol layer that allows the different components to talk to each other, and then an application layer whereby users interact with the internet via e-mail, web browsing, instant messaging, etc. It is the separation of layers which Zittrain sees as crucial as it allows engineers, developers and innovators to work on the area they are specialists in without having to be experts in layers above or below them. The creator of the next successful social networking or internet search service does not need to have a detailed understanding of internet transport protocols or ask permission of the organizations that manage domain name servers or IP address allocations. These functions are independent of each other to the extent that control is distributed preventing any single organization from dictating who can gain access or what the network can be used for. His term for the defining feature of the internet, which has sparked such innovation across the communications and publishing industries, is 'generative':

> Generativity is a system's capacity to produce unanticipated change through unfiltered contributions from broad and varied audiences.
>
> (Zittrain, 2008)

The internet has a high capacity for generating new services because it is a relatively open and freely accessible platform, which allows the creativity of others to flourish. We have seen earlier in this chapter how its predecessors such as Compuserve and AOL operated closed networks where users were only able to access services approved by the network owners. Such systems were not conducive to generating innovative services as there was a corporate filter that prevented most third-party developers from entering. It is the 'unanticipated' part of Zittrain's definition above that is perhaps most significant: accurately predicting future technological developments is impossible, as to predict a new invention is effectively the same as inventing it. If anyone had anticipated the wheel before the first one had been made then they could be seen as its inventor. Similarly, in 1993 who could have foreseen how the web would have developed and the services that it spawned? Zittrain cites Wikipedia as an example of an unlikely service that has become a global resource used by hundreds of millions of people every week. Who would have anticipated that an online encyclopaedia which relies on unpaid and unvetted amateurs to produce its entries would become a primary reference source? Would anyone have imagined that a 19-year-old student would develop a social networking service while still at university that within seven years was regularly used by 800 million people? Had Compuserve or indeed any other proprietary network had a say in those developments then it is unlikely they would ever have emerged.

However, Zittrain points to threats on the horizon to the generative capacity of the internet to stimulate future innovations. Some of these centre on the characteristics of modern internet devices and appliances which are less open to hosting applications than a PC, and this will be looked at in the next chapter on information consumption. More relevant to our discussion here on information distribution are threats to the open nature of the internet as a platform for the free movement of digital bits. Whereas the ISPs, which transport internet traffic from web servers to end-users, have generally been agnostic as to what the data packets contain and given equal preference to Google's packets as any of its competitors, this may be changing. Network neutrality is the term that defines this notion of equal carriage and it has been a topic of heated debate amongst academics, legislators and network operators for several years. There is a fear that without adequate competition among providers of internet connectivity there may be a temptation for some companies to favour certain online services at the expense of others. Where an ISP is also a provider of telecommunication voice services, such as BT in the UK and AT&T in the USA, it is possible to see why they might not look very favourably on competing services such as Skype and Google Voice. Under those circumstances it might be tempting for some ISPs to degrade or block internet telephony services. In 2005 in the USA a small telecommunications operator, Madison River Communication, was found guilty by the regulator of preventing its internet customers from accessing internet telephony provider Vonage and fined $15,000. While this might be seen as evidence that, in the USA at least, regulators are enforcing the maintenance of a neutral and generative internet, there are growing arguments that new rules for internet governance need to be developed to prevent the subtle chipping away by commercial interests at the network. For publishers and information providers, the stakes are high as they come to depend increasingly on an open internet to distribute their content. Imagine the implications of a major media and news provider such as News Corporation entering into a commercial arrangement with a dominant ISP in the UK such as Virgin Media or BT. It would be technically possible for the ISP to give preference to News Corporation traffic and slow down traffic from its competitors such as the BBC or the Guardian Media Group. Over time this might discourage visitors to those sites as they find them less accessible than those from News Corporation. Of course, this is a hypothetical situation but not an unrealistic one. In 2010 the UK Communications Minister, Ed Vaizey, was reported by Halliday (2010) as arguing in a conference speech that ISPs should be able to abandon network neutrality and allowed to provide preferential service to content providers that pay for it. While arguing on the one hand for an open internet, the minister also stated:

> We have got to continue to encourage the market to innovate and experiment with different business models and ways of providing consumers with what they want. This could include the evolution of a two sided market where consumers and content providers could choose to pay for differing levels of quality of service.
>
> (Halliday, 2010)

For information professionals the implications of a move to a more tiered level of service provision and pricing should be concerning. The relatively even playing field that the internet has provided for information providers of all sizes has been a significant and positive development for information professionals. Never before has so much information been so freely available to so many and any developments which might take us back to a less open and more restrictive environment should be examined closely.

Concluding comments

This chapter has shown how new technologies are transforming the ways information is being distributed and the impact it is having on information creators, mediators and users. The internet is reconfiguring the information value chain and creating new opportunities for content creators to communicate directly with end consumers. Mobile networks are allowing users to break free of the constraints of buildings whether the home, office or the library, and the deployment of fourth generation mobile networks over the coming years will only accelerate this process as wireless download speeds could reach 1 Gbit/s. It is forecast that global mobile data traffic will increase tenfold between 2011 and 2015 to 6 million terabytes a month (Cisco 2011). The following chapter considers where all this data will end up and looks at the ways that users are consuming information, the devices and systems they are using and what uses the information is being put to.

QUESTIONS TO THINK ABOUT

1. How real is the threat of disintermediation of library and information professionals by the internet?
2. Is online piracy inevitable in a digital world and something that content producers need to get used to and adapt their business models accordingly?
3. Does WikiLeaks strengthen democracy or threaten it?
4. How significant is Zittrain's notion of the internet as possessing generative capabilities in explaining its rapid and widespread adoption?

CHAPTER 5
New models of information consumption

Introduction

Having looked at new ways that information is produced, distributed and stored, this chapter will consider new ways that we are consuming information. Ultimately, the way we consume information has not changed over the years as it still relies on the sensory functions of our eyes and ears to pass sights and sounds to our brains for decoding, processing and making sense of. However, the methods and devices by which information now reaches us have changed dramatically. An evolving ecosystem of hardware and software is constantly struggling for our attention as we work, play, relax and travel. Where time and location were once constraints on the types of information we could access, these barriers are being broken down as devices become portable and networks become pervasive. Giddens (1990) explained the significance of this dislocation with his concept of time and space distanciation whereby remote connections and interactions come to dominate modern life. The first telegraph and telephone systems built in the 19th century began this revolution while more recent developments in computing and mobile devices and networks have accelerated it.

The following sections will explore a range of issues surrounding these developments and consider their implications for information professionals and the work they do. The plethora of new information consumption devices will be examined within the context of the networks and information ecosystems that support them. A central theme will be the tension between organizations that are attempting to exert control over these systems and those organizations and users looking to develop a more open environment. This tension is an extension of the battles we have seen over PC operating systems and which now extend to mobile devices and the applications that run on them. We will look at the discussions surrounding information overload and how, as some would argue, we are becoming unable to process all the information that is pushed at us from fellow workers and social media contacts. Related to these discussions is the issue of information literacy and a concern that, while most of us can use the internet to find information, many people struggle to make sense of what we find. The opportunities for information professionals in helping users to develop their information literacy skills will be considered, as the role for many IPs is changing from information gatekeeper to facilitator. Finally, this chapter will look at how organizations are trying to make sense of the information that flows through their networks and consider whether the promises of knowledge management advocates from the late 20th century are finally being realized.

Information consumption devices

Perhaps the most visible evidence of the digital information revolution of the last 20 years is the devices through which we access these digital streams. This really got under way in the 1980s with the mass deployment of PCs on workers' desktops and then into households. Vasquez and Shiffler (2011) estimate that the installed global base of PCs was 1.4 billion in 2010 and will rise to 2.3 billion by 2015. Before the rise of the internet most PCs were either standalone devices or operated within a closed organizational network. Most of the information they processed was generated within the organization or household by the user or others on the network and consisted primarily of text documents or spreadsheets. Information professionals were among the first to access information remotely through the use of online databases and aggregators such as Dialog, Orbit and Questel. However, the complexities of creating a network connection, structuring search commands and the expense of subscriptions restricted their use to libraries and research institutes. A middle ground emerged in the 1990s when CD-ROMs emerged as a suitable media for end-user searching. A number of database providers offered their information on CDs that did not require networked computers and, while often expensive to purchase, removed the danger of inexperienced searchers running up large connection and download charges. While a number of information vendors still offer CDs of their collections, that media as well as traditional dial-up access to online databases have been eclipsed by the internet as a distribution network and the world wide web as an interface to integrate online resources.

As we will see later in this chapter, these developments have had significant implications for many information professionals as access to online information has been opened up to the masses. However, equally interesting is the lesson it provides for the benefits of open systems at the expense of more closed environments in terms of stimulating the diffusion of innovations. In the early days of online databases in the 1970s and 1980s, dedicated software and, very often, hardware were required to access the databases. On top of these requirements, the process for dialling in to the databases was often complicated and involved going through data gateways on the public telecommunications network. Once connected, the user had to use specific search terms and syntax that varied between databases with the result that most information professionals tended to focus on interrogating databases they were familiar with. The proprietary nature of these online systems restricted their diffusion throughout organizations and it was not until a more open platform emerged in the form of the PC and the internet that online information became available to more end-users. The PC represented a multi-tasking device while the internet offered an open network to a range of data services beyond those offered by monopolistic telecommunications operators.

The evolution of the PC itself is a demonstration of how a relatively open system can win over a more closed one. The history of the PC and the battles between Microsoft and Apple over how a personal computer should operate are well documented, but it is worth reminding ourselves why for most of the last 30 years the PC, based on a Microsoft operating system, has been the dominant paradigm in personal computing. While Apple in late 2011 was, for a short while, one of the most valuable companies on the planet, it should be remembered that in the 1990s the company was nearly forced out of the computing business. By the early 1990s the company had squandered its early lead in the personal computing sector by sticking to a closed model whereby the company sought to control the hardware and the software that ran on it. As a consequence, the range of Apple computers on the market was very limited as was the software they could run, while personal computers running Microsoft's MS-DOS and then Windows dominated the desktop.

Key to the success of Microsoft was the fact that no single company had a monopoly on making PCs, which were made from standard, interchangeable components. This encouraged hundreds of companies to start making PCs, driving down prices and stimulating innovation as they sought to produce better machines. The only monopoly was centred on the operating system with Microsoft taking a licence fee for every legal copy of MS-DOS and Windows in use. Even though many would argue that Apple offered a superior product, the significantly lower price and wider choice of PCs made them far more attractive to purchasers. Once an organization started using PCs and the associated software, they became less likely to switch to another system such as the Apple Mac, creating a virtuous circle for Microsoft where the more people who used its software, the harder it became for a competitor to make inroads into the market. Organizations that have invested in training their employees on one operating system will be reluctant to incur the costs of training them in another. These dynamics also work in the consumer market for technology where users become familiar with operating environments and are often resistant to change.

Mobile consumption devices

The PC coupled with the internet introduced the masses to online information consumption but it is the more recent developments in mobile technologies that are changing the expectations that many of us have about where and when information should be made available. Modern smartphones and tablet devices contain more processing power than a PC of only a few years ago and, by their nature, can be used in a far wider range of locations and situations. Figure 5.1 shows the relative global penetration of these devices by the end of 2011 but, more interestingly, it also shows the speed with which they have been adopted.

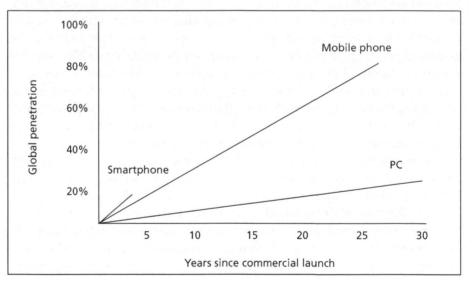

Figure 5.1 Speed of adoption of new technologies (2011)

Perhaps the first thing to notice from Figure 5.1 is the speed at which the mobile phone has been adopted in comparison to the PC. While it has taken 30 years since the launch of the first mass-market IBM PC to achieve a global penetration of 24%, the mobile phone has been adopted by 84 out of every 100 people in the world in slightly less time. Smartphones, although a subset of the broader mobile phone market, are being taken up at an even faster rate. Four years after the launch of the first Apple iPhone in 2007, smartphones were being used by approximately 16% of the global population and, according to J. Williams (2011), accounted for 25% of all mobile sales in 2011. It is likely that by 2015 most new mobile phones will be 'smart', with the consequence that the term 'smartphone' will become meaningless. Increasingly, the same will be true of the term 'PC' as devices such as computers, tablets and phones become less distinct and, for some purposes, start to replace each other. This will have significant implications for device manufacturers such as HP, the world's largest manufacturer of PCs, signified when it announced in 2011 that it was considering whether to remain in the PC business. IBM, the company that launched the first modern PC in 1981, sold off its PC business to Chinese manufacturer Lenovo in 2004. However, it is the implications of the mass take-up of new portable devices for information consumption that is of most interest here.

According to the UK's Office for National Statistics (ONS, 2011) in 2011 there were 17.6 million mobile phone internet users across the UK with 6 million people accessing the internet over their phone for the first time during the previous 12 months. These figures represent a doubling over the previous year and illustrate a dramatic change in how many people are accessing the internet. According to the same report, 77% of all UK households had internet access, which primarily came from fixed line connections over telephone and cable television networks. However, within those households a large proportion will have set up wi-fi networks to allow a range of devices to share the fixed internet connection. The ONS (2011) also estimates that 93% of internet households were using broadband connections instead of the older and slower dial-up method. Across most of the developed world these numbers are broadly similar with northern European countries tending to have the highest broad band penetration rates (OECD, 2011). So what does this mean for how information enters the household? The key points are that most of us now have high-speed, always-on and, thanks to wi-fi and mobile broadband, mobile access to the internet. Therefore, two key parts of the infrastructure required for a true information society are in place both at work and in the home: the networks to carry the information and the devices to present it to us. While these networks will offer ever-faster connection speeds and the devices will become cheaper and more powerful, it is the final layer of the services that run over them which will be of most interest, particularly to information professionals. In Chapter 2 we saw how new content creators were emerging to take advantage of the digital information revolution and it is in the application layer that sits on top of these consumption devices that interesting developments are taking place.

Looking beyond the artefact

The digital revolution has spawned a plethora of devices that allow us to create, share and consume information in a variety of formats. Perhaps it was the launch of the iPod in 2001 that showed us what was possible when digitized and compressed content, in this case music, was combined with portable micro-electronics. Apple's advertising at the time promised 'a thousand songs in your pocket', which was a radical departure from the commonly used portable cassette or CD players, which could only hold a single music album at a time. While we now take it for granted that our music collections can go with us wherever we are, the iPod and similar devices broke down the restrictions of physical media such as tapes and CDs where there was a strong correlation between size and content. A tape-based Sony Walkman could never be any smaller than the audio cassette whereas digital music devices have become smaller while also increasing the amount of content they can store. Apple's largest capacity iPod by late 2011 offered 160 gigabytes of storage, enough for 40,000 music tracks. Increasingly, even these devices are becoming redundant as smartphones become the preferred choice for listening to music on the move. However, while much media attention is focused on the shiny new devices that Apple, Samsung, HTC and others are flooding our shops with, it is important to look beyond the hardware and at the software and content distribution systems that power them. Apple was not the first manufacturer of portable, digital music players but it was the first company to offer a device that linked to an easy-to-use and free piece of software, iTunes, which made transferring music from CD collections to the device a simple process. In 2003 the company also made it easier for consumers to buy and legally download digital music via the iTunes software, which extended the utility of Apple devices at the expense of the competition. Producing the best portable music player was no longer enough; it needed to be linked to software that allowed users' music collections to be managed via the PC and some form of online music store. Apple got this right at the beginning and effectively locked out its competitors through the use of proprietary software, exclusive deals with the music industry and its variation of the AAC music compression format FairPlay. The company's success with this approach was quickly realized with iPods accounting for almost 90% of the US market by 2004 (Betteridge, 2004) and the term 'iPod' becoming a generic term for all such devices, similar to 'Hoover' for vacuum cleaners.

While iPods and similar devices have a fairly narrow range of uses in terms of information consumption, primarily audio and video content, the newer generation of smartphones and tablet computers can present a broader range of content. In some ways they are becoming the Swiss army knives of the digital age by encroaching on the territory of digital still and video cameras, music and video players and some of the functions of the PC. The technical wizardry that allows devices weighing little more than 100 grams to shoot high definition video, store thousands of music tracks, surf the internet as well as make phone calls is impressive and an important factor for users' purchasing decisions. However, longer term commercial success for device manufacturers will be driven by factors they may have less control over. These include the operating systems that power their devices and which, to a large extent, control the user interface. By early 2012 there were five main smartphone software platforms: Apple's iOS, Google's Android, Microsoft's Windows Phone, RIM's BlackBerry and Nokia's Symbian. Apple, and RIM's systems are similar in that the companies also manufacture the hardware, creating a tightly integrated experience for users. Android, on the other hand, is an open source software project allowing any hardware manufacturer to produce devices on which the software can run. Microsoft's operating system sits somewhere between the above two models with hardware manufacturers able to license the software for running on their devices. The Symbian platform was Nokia's attempt to create an open source system for smartphones, which did not meet with the same success as Android. In 2011 Nokia reverted to maintaining Symbian as a proprietary platform and in the same year announced it would be focusing on developing handsets for the Windows operating system. For information professionals this presents a fascinating opportunity to observe how an important component of the emerging information society will develop. Will Apple make the same mistake it did in the 1980s with its Mac computer when it tried to control the hardware and the software? Will Microsoft be able to replicate the success it had with its PC operating system by focusing on the software and leaving the hardware for others, particularly Nokia, to manufacture? Will the more open Android system allow Google to become a central point of reference for mobile users as it has done on our desktop?

Table 5.1 provides an overview of the smartphone market at the end of 2011 in terms of the operating systems, hardware and associated third party

Table 5.1 Global smartphone market (end 2011)

Operating system	Market share	Market share annual change	Third party apps	Handsets	Handset manufacturers
Android	47%	+110%	300,000	80+	25+
iOS	20%	+20%	500,000	3	1
Symbian	12%	–50%	50,000	10	4
BlackBerry	11%	–20%	30,000	22	1
Windows Phone	2%	n/a	35,000	20+	8
Other	8%	n/a	n/a	n/a	n/a

applications. While the Symbian and BlackBerry platforms can be seen to have lost market share between 2010 and 2011, Android and iOS have experienced significant growth with more phones running Android than any other operating system. There are a number of factors behind the success of Google's platform, which first became available on a phone a year after the launch of the iPhone. While the backing of Google has been a key driver of success, perhaps a more important reason was the decision to open source the operating system, allowing others to expand and extend the software as well as build their own configurations of hardware. While only Apple can make iPhones, there are more than 25 companies that make Android phones. Some argue that this creates confusion amongst consumers as the experience of using an Android handset will be inconsistent across different devices. However, the converse of this is that competition amongst manufacturers to produce better phones will encourage innovation on the platform. The market shares in Table 5.1 clearly indicate that Google's approach has paid off and, whereas open source operating systems for the desktop PC have never taken off, an open source platform for mobile devices seems to be popular with consumers.

It's all about the apps

To be successful in the smartphone market a high-quality, feature-rich handset and an intuitive and responsive operating system are essential. However, while those two characteristics are necessary they are no longer sufficient to ensure success. A third feature is a well populated app store where third party software developers can upload the applications they have written for that platform and users can browse for free or low-cost downloads. Apple pioneered this concept in 2008 with the launch of its iTunes app store, which by the end of 2011 hosted over half a million applications. Google's Android Marketplace was not far behind with more than 300,000 apps. It is here that Apple has conceded that a relatively open system for encouraging the development of software is a benefit both to itself and its users. While the company sets rules for developers on how the apps must integrate with the iPhone, and vets new titles before releasing them through the iTunes store, Apple has created a software ecosystem which by the middle of 2011 had seen more than 15 billion apps being downloaded (Rao, 2011). As well as encouraging the wider use of the iOS platform and iPhones, the app store is also a major source of revenue for the company, with Apple taking a 30% commission for paid apps.

Developing a successful application environment is critical for new entrants into the market and something that Microsoft will be very aware of.

Launching its Windows Phone operating system several years after Apple's and Google's platforms, Microsoft has put a lot of resources behind encouraging outside developers to create versions of their software for its phones. However, as with many software platforms there is the issue of scale whereby developers will focus their efforts on operating systems that are widely used and neglect those they believe have no future. This is similar to the notion of network effects observed across many information and communication networks: the value of the network to its users increases with the number of users on the network. Although the dynamics are slightly different when applied to application development, the principles are broadly similar with the possibility of a 'winner takes all' outcome similar to that experienced by Microsoft with its PC operating systems throughout the 1980s and 1990s.

CASE STUDY – AMAZON

The online retailer Amazon has steadily built itself up from its launch as an online bookseller in 1995 to be the internet's largest department store, with a market value of more than $100 billion by late 2011 and annual sales of over $40 billion. Since 2005 the company has expanded its product range from books to include electrical goods, clothes, downloadable music and videos as well as creating a marketplace for other retailers to sell items. In this respect it can be viewed as a department store that sells items itself but also rents out space to in-store concessions. However, for information professionals its most important innovations have been in its integration of digital content and hardware devices for content consumption. Following Apple's success in reinventing music consumption with the iPod, Amazon has made a similar move for e-books. Its Kindle e-book reader has been an enormous success for the company and will sell an estimated 26 million of the devices in 2012, up from 17.5 million in 2011 (Yarrow, 2011). In mid-2011 Amazon announced it was selling more e-books in the USA than paper copies for the first time, leading the company's founder, Jeff Bezos, to comment: 'We had high hopes that this would happen eventually, but we never imagined it would happen this quickly – we've been selling print books for 15 years and Kindle books for less than four years' (Gabbatt, 2011). While e-books and e-book readers have existed in various forms since the 1980s, it is the Kindle that has finally brought them into the mainstream. The success is a combination of the e-Ink technology in the devices that mimic the light-reflective qualities of paper and the Amazon online store, which makes purchasing and downloading books wirelessly a simple task. The launch of the colour screen tablet device, the Kindle Fire in late 2011 signifies a move by Amazon into other forms of content distribution via dedicated devices, particularly video and rich media. It seems that Amazon and Apple are on similar paths to create more vertically integrated technology and content distribution companies, developments that have significant implications for information consumers of all types.

Information ecosystems: gilded cages or innovation hotbeds?

We've seen how two of the most successful technology companies, Apple and Amazon (see case study above), have created profitable businesses by making digital content easier for end-users to access and consume. Through their integration of e-commerce, software and well designed hardware they have managed to dominate the online music and e-book markets respectively. Apple's app store has encouraged thousands of independent software developers to create applications which, in some cases, have made their creators rich. The Amazon Kindle provides a platform for anyone, with or without a contract from a publisher, to have their written works offered for sale. While the most successful Kindle titles are generally by mainstream writers who were already successful in the world of paper books, some new authors have managed to achieve hundreds of thousands of downloads without having a high profile in the traditional publishing world. John Locke has managed to sell more than a million copies of his books through the Kindle channel without going through a publisher or ever selling a paper copy of any of his titles. He puts his success down to writing good page turners combined with an aggressive pricing strategy. Rather than the average $10 that publishers were charging for similar e-books he decided to charge only 99 cents, on the assumption that his margins would be lower but higher sales would more than make up for that. Drawing on his commercial experience, Locke was attracted to the commission structure that Amazon offered:

> I've been in commission sales all my life, and when I learned Kindle and the other e-book platforms offered a royalty of 35 per cent on books priced at 99 cents, I couldn't believe it. To most people, 35 cents doesn't sound like much. To me, it seemed like a license to print money.

> (Barnett and Alleyne, 2011)

While competing on price has worked for Locke it is not clear how sustainable such an approach would be for authors of less popular titles. However, it is undeniable that the Kindle platform has allowed him and other authors to exert more control over how their works are published. Established publishers can be bypassed, stripping costs out of the book publishing value chain and allowing authors to keep more of the cover price and readers to pay less for the titles they buy. For proponents of the free flow of information and the democratization of ideas this seems like a positive move as barriers to information production and consumption are broken down. However, there may be a price to pay for this digital nirvana and by the time this happens, it may be too late to do anything about it.

The e-books that Amazon sells for its Kindle devices are in a proprietary format, AZW, which contains a digital rights management (DRM) element restricting what can be done with the e-book. These restrictions include the number of devices that users can read their downloaded titles on and the ability to lend copies to other Kindle owners. Apple imposed similar restrictions until 2009 on music downloaded from their iTunes store, which capped the number of iPods any individual user could play their music on. Content owners, whether music or book publishers, have often insisted on the use of DRM to protect their copyrighted material before agreeing to distribution deals with companies like Apple and Amazon. This is understandable when they can see the illegal downloading of their artists' works on a mass scale via P2P networks. The software industry has used similar measures such as unique product keys to try and control use of their products by non-paying users for many years. So while there is a business logic to restricting what users can do with content they have downloaded, it presents a number of challenges to several established practices in the publishing world: fair dealing, resale and lending.

Fair dealing

Although its interpretation within the law varies between countries there is a general principle across most developed economies that copyright law needs to be flexible enough to allow certain exceptions. These exceptions typically relate to uses of copyrighted material for research, journalism, review and criticism. In its strictest sense, most intellectual property laws give control over what can be done with copyrighted materials to the copyright owner. A literal interpretation of the law could, for example, prevent a writer, musician or film maker from allowing negative reviews of his/her book, opera or film from being published where extracts of the work were used to illustrate the review. Similarly, academic writers would need to obtain permission from any other author they were citing within their own writing. For librarians, copyright laws, strictly enforced, would prevent library users from photocopying extracts of books or journals without permission of the copyright owner. Clearly, the enforcement of such rules would restrict intellectual discourse, academic research and basic journalism. It is for these reasons that the principle of fair dealing or fair use have emerged, whereby exceptions to copyright law are allowed to permit the exchange of ideas and the furthering of knowledge through development of the intellectual commons. In the UK this has typically been interpreted as allowing the copying of a single chapter of a book or an article from a journal for the purpose of research. However, the implementation of some DRM solutions to digital information has circumvented the fair dealing tradition by preventing even the modest copying of extracts of published works. In the case of the Kindle there are limitations imposed by the nature of the device itself; making a photocopy of a page on a Kindle is obviously rather difficult but, because it is a standalone device, copying text from the hardware onto a computer is also restricted. DRM within the e-books held on the Kindle also places restrictions on how much text can be exported and this amount can be set at zero, depending on the wishes of the publisher.

Copyright reformer and academic Lawrence Lessig revealed how DRM solutions can be implemented in a way that sweeps aside the notion of fair use with a few clicks of the mouse. In 2001 he was looking at an Adobe Acrobat e-book version of an out-of-copyright edition of *Alice's Adventures in Wonderland*, when he noticed that Adobe had set the permissions for copying sections of the text to, 'No text selections can be copied from this book to the clipboard' (Lessig, 2001). Even if this edition had still been in copyright the principle of fair use would have applied but for a copy that was outside the copyright term such a restriction made no sense. While Lessig's example might seem trivial it demonstrates the power that DRM restrictions can place on content that would not be possible in the analogue world.

Resale

While copyright owners across most economies are free to set the price at which the outputs of their creative endeavours are sold in the marketplace, this right is removed if the original purchaser decides to resell the book or music album. That, at least, has been the accepted practice across Europe and even enshrined in US copyright legislation. We probably don't even think about this aspect of intellectual property law and take it for granted that once we have purchased a legal copy of a book it is up to us what we do with it. It is hard to imagine having to seek the permission of the book's author or publisher before being able to sell it to our local book dealer or on eBay. However, applying these practices to the digital world is a little more complicated as the music files on our iPod or books on our Kindle create new problems for copyright owners. While some publishers might resent not receiving a percentage of the income from second-hand book sales they can at least take comfort from the fact that a paper book can only be read by one person at a time. Digital copies of books and music, on the other hand, can be transferred between readers and listeners while still allowing the original purchaser to retain his or her copy. This obviously underpins the core rationale for DRM but it also stifles the resale market. With the Kindle, for example, the terms and conditions plainly state that, 'Unless otherwise specified, Digital Content is licensed, not sold, to you by the Content Provider' (Amazon, 2011). This represents a fundamental shift in the relationship between publishers and readers and removes the right to sell on copies of works bought in the Kindle market. While it may be publishers and not Amazon who have driven this change in the sale of digital content, it is a landmark development that will have repercussions throughout the information sector and something we will come back to later in this chapter when we explore the notion of content renting rather than ownership. Even if the implications for information consumption are not as significant as this, it certainly spells trouble for second-hand bookshops.

Lending

At the heart of libraries of all kinds is the principle of lending materials, traditionally books, to users. From their foundations in the 19th century, public libraries around the world have sought to make reading matter available to those who could not afford to purchase books, journals or newspapers. Although the arrangements vary across countries, public lending rights have ensured authors receive compensation for the copies lent by libraries. Just as with the first sale principle described above, purchasers of books have been free to lend them to whoever they wish without requiring the permission of the copyright owner. While many libraries, public, academic and commercial, are incorporating e-books into their collections and grappling with the technical and legal issues of how they can be lent out, the situation is more complex for end-users. Amazon, as the world's largest retailer of e-books, is worth looking at again in this context with its terms and conditions stating:

> Unless specifically indicated otherwise, you may not sell, rent, lease, distribute, broadcast, sublicense, or otherwise assign any rights to the Digital Content or any portion of it to any third party.
>
> (Amazon, 2011)

In the USA it is possible, if the publisher permits, to loan a Kindle e-book to someone else for 14 days during which time the loaner is not able to read it. However, this does not seem to apply in other countries and the 14 day limit is rather restrictive.

So far this chapter has explored some of the business models that technology and content producers have been experimenting with when developing new models of information consumption. We have seen how Apple, Google and Amazon are attempting to integrate the hardware and software powering the digital devices that provide access to these new information superstores. At the same time these companies are also trying to encourage thriving ecosystems of developers to add value to the information consumption experience through app stores. However, we have also considered the potential downside to these innovations as content owners place new restrictions on what we can do with the information we have downloaded and the implications this might have for end-users and information professionals. The following section looks at some of the competing forces and technologies that may result in a less digitally locked-down future, which may be closer to the original aim of the world wide web's creator, Tim Berners-Lee, and his vision of it being a force for positive social change.

Returning to an open web

While the symbols of the digital revolution may be the smartphones, tablets and laptops that we carry with us, underpinning the radical changes to how we create, distribute and consume information over the last 20 years have been the internet and the world wide web. The internet has provided a relatively open platform across which digital information of all types can flow while the world wide web has given us an intuitive interface to interact with the information. Without those two developments, the shiny gadgets we crave and proudly show our friends would be useless objects, not able to access the music, films, e-books and other online content that gives them meaning. In Chapter 4 we saw how the open standards that define the internet and the world wide web have created a hotbed for innovation of all sorts, which would not have been possible had a commercial entity been in control of access both for content creators and consumers. In some ways, the success of Apple and Amazon in the music and book publishing arenas represent attempts to pull back power from the anarchy of the open web and to control what can flow over the network and how such information is used. For some this has been a positive development as the user experience is tightly defined and allows less technically minded consumers, probably most of us, to pay for a generally fault-free consumption experience. However, there is a danger that by forfeiting some of the messiness of a more open web in exchange for easier access to the content we want we may be undermining the future of the web itself.

We have seen how the plethora of apps for mobile devices has been a key driver of smartphone adoption since 2008. The utility value of such phones and tablets increases with each new app as they extend the uses to which they can be put. Social networking apps allow users to easily keep in touch with friends, mapping apps integrated with GPS help us find our way and content apps make consuming news and entertainment information a smoother experience than clicking across multiple web pages. While a discrete app may be a logical method for achieving a task such as navigation or document creation, in the same way that we use specific software applications on our PCs to perform similar tasks, it presents problems when apps are used for information consumption. On a PC the web browser has become the dominant tool for accessing online information because it is a content-neutral device that will present any information so long as it conforms to the open standards of the world wide web. We do not need to use separate browsers or applications to read information created by different publishers. The *Guardian* newspaper online can be read just as easily within any web browser as the *New York Times* online. However, the increasing use of apps by publishers presents a challenge to this situation, which could ultimately reduce the information choices of device users. Publishers, particularly in the magazine and newspaper sectors, are seeing sales of their printed editions steadily reducing as consumers spend more time looking for information on the internet. Maintaining content-rich websites has become the norm for such companies as they try to find ways to develop online revenue streams. Carrying advertisements on these websites is the most common way of generating income but keeping visitors on their sites is always a problem when a competitor's content is only a click away. The walled garden of a dedicated app is one way of holding on to online readers as the publisher's content can be presented in a closed environment. However, some commentators such as Zittrain (2008) see the increasing use of these apps for content distribution as a regressive step in the evolution of the information society. Creating information islands that do not communicate with each other via web links, it is argued, will take us back to the pre-world wide web age of Compuserve and AOL. For information professionals this should be a concern as it has been the free linking between web pages that has advanced the creation, distribution and consumption of information more than any other invention since the invention of the printing press.

HTML5 – an antidote to appification?

Is the Balkanization of the world wide web through the widespread development and adoption of apps an inevitability or can something be done about it? Many argue that the fifth generation of the HTML web markup language, HTML5, promises salvation from a fragmented web. Although still under development in late 2011, it is the first new version of HTML since HTML4 in 1997. HTML5 offers a number of improved features and innovations for web developers, with significant improvements in how it manages multimedia such as video and audio and the ability to work with cached, offline data among the most important. Developers are currently taking advantage of these features to create HTML5 apps that can work across PC and smartphone platforms. Such apps have the appearance of a discrete application but are run within the traditional web browser. The advantages for developers are: the app only needs to written once and will work across any device capable of running a modern web browser; content presented within HTML5 is indexable by search engines and so can be found by users; as with traditional HTML, content can be mashed with other sources to create information-rich pages; and the bottleneck of the app store can be circumvented as HTML5 content can be distributed across the open web. For publishers the cross-platform compatibility of HTML5 means cost-savings in application development, which allows more resources to be put into creating better content. Opening up content to search engines can result in higher visitor numbers, which could be seen as a counter to the attraction, to some publishers, of traditional apps as walled gardens where they have more control over how their information is consumed. Whether HTML lives up to the expectations of its proponents will take several years to be realized but the economic benefits it promises to publishers and the visibility it offers to search engines should make it an attractive development platform. Burley (2011) expands on the challenges that publishers face with respect to repackaging their content for the tablet and smartphone era and the need to offer consumers more than just the same information in a fancy new package:

> For publishers this means knowing and anticipating audience needs, having a thorough understanding of all available content, including content from public databases, and having a nimble infrastructure that allows disparate types of content to be 'mashed together'.
>
> (Burley, 2011)

Burley's suggestion that publishers should make better use of third party information to create value-added mashups is not a new one but is radical in that it requires a different mindset from the traditional publishing model, which focuses on control over published outputs. In Chapter 4 we saw how public sector bodies are becoming more proactive in making their data available for others to use and, as Burley recommends, publishers might do well to integrate this information into their offerings. The opportunities are significant, particularly where publishers combine the value of such information with the functionality of new mobile devices.

We can begin to see how this might work with the rise of augmented reality mobile services such as Layar and Google Goggles. These new applications make use of the location awareness through GPS, cameras and internet connections on smartphones to interpret what the user can see via the phone camera. A simple example of the capability of Google Goggles, for example, would be to hold a phone running the application up to a famous landmark such as St Paul's Cathedral in London or the Sydney Opera House and it would match the image to similar ones in the Google image index and then present information from a variety of sources about the building. More relevant to content owners, the Paperboy app works with publishers to allow users to take a photo of a page in a magazine or newspaper and then share it with friends or be shown similar content from other publications. These applications are, at the beginning of 2012, still in an embryonic stage but they demonstrate that the technology works and, as devices become more powerful, perhaps offers opportunities for publishers to find new ways of presenting their content. A challenge for information professionals will be to keep up to speed with these developments and be able to discern which have value for their users.

Rent or buy?

This is a question that has faced those looking for a home for generations. It is also increasingly becoming a question for information consumers as the options for accessing content, particularly entertainment, increase. For the first 30 or so years of television we only had the option to watch programmes as they were broadcast with no accessible mechanism for recording video content to watch later. Since the 1980s we have been able to rent or buy video cassettes and then DVDs as well as record programmes on our own devices. Similarly, books have been available to buy in shops or borrow from libraries. Like television programmes, music was accessible over the airwaves or could be bought in the form of records, tapes or CDs. For those producing entertainment content, whether film, music, video or printed, the period since World War 2 has generally been a profitable one. As we have seen in previous chapters, the channels for distribution were limited and the ability of consumers to circumvent those channels restricted by the analogue technologies of the day. However, the digitization of both the content and the networks that carry it have opened up new opportunities to break free of previous constraints. For the music industry this has led to the illegal downloading of billions of music tracks, which, according to many in the industry, has decimated the recording sector. The figures are stark: a 33% decline in recorded music sales in the UK between 2001 and 2011 and a 50% decline in the USA (Economist, 2011). While iTunes and other legal music downloading services have provided welcome revenue streams for publishers, they have not made up for the declining revenues delivered by falling CD sales.

Perhaps the future for content industries lies not in trying to replicate the past with digital business models that mimic how we used to consume information. While iTunes is a very different way of purchasing music, it still rests of the assumption that consumers wish to own their digital purchases. For some this is undoubtedly the case but an increasing number of consumers seem happy to move away from the ownership model to one that is more transient. Content streaming services have been gaining in popularity, particularly for music. These include services such as Pandora, Last.fm and Spotify whereby users have access to hundreds of thousands of music tracks that can be streamed over the internet to PCs and mobile devices. Spotify is perhaps the most interesting of the services in that it offers a hybrid model whereby its users have access to streaming millions of tracks and paying subscribers can even download up to 3333 tracks onto portable devices for playing offline. However, these downloaded tracks can only be played as long as the user continues to pay the monthly subscription fee. In effect, the service is like a radio station that allows the listener to choose what is played. Social elements of many of the streaming services show users what their 'friends' are listening to and even suggests music that they might like based on their listening history.

In Chapter 4 we considered the economics of these services for both publishers and artists, and the revenues from streaming looked very different from those generated by CD sales. However, from an information consumption perspective the rise of streaming services presents some interesting challenges to how we think about the ownership of content. We have already seen that purchasers of e-books on the Kindle platform do not own a copy of the book in the same way they do with paper copies but, rather, are licensing the content. Music and video streaming extends this further with the content, for most subscribers, passing through their devices and only existing to the user for the length of the playback. For users, a major benefit of streamed content is access to far larger libraries than they could ever own if they had to pay for and download each track or video. For content owners it presents the opportunity to overcome digital piracy albeit generating smaller revenues on their assets than in the pre-internet era.

Making sense of it all

We know that the world has never before been presented with so much information and being able to keep on top of the demands it places on us, as well as sort the wheat from the chaff, is a growing problem for information professionals and the end-users they serve. Before the arrival of PCs on every desktop and then their connection to the internet, information professionals were often the gatekeepers to information resources. Now that role is changing to being more of a guide and teacher, helping users navigate and find the information themselves.

Information literacy

Anyone who works in education will have a view on the impact the internet has had on how young people learn. Some will bemoan the rise of the Wikipedia generation, which finds instant information gratification from a Google search, while others point to the richness of the resources to which students now have access at home and school. In recent years there has been a growing debate about the longer-term impacts that the internet is having on how all of us think about information and ideas. Some such as Carr (2010) believe that there is a downside to having so much information on tap and that it is diminishing our ability to think more deeply about ideas and concepts as we flit from one web page to another. In 2008 in *The Atlantic* magazine Carr provocatively titled his article 'Is Google making us stupid? What the internet is doing to our brains', which questioned whether in our embrace of the web we are losing the important faculty of critical thinking. Carr's account of how he uses the internet as a resource is honest and chimes with many of us who can remember a pre-internet age:

> For more than a decade now, I've been spending a lot of time online, searching and surfing and sometimes adding to the great databases of the Internet. The Web has been a godsend to me as a writer. Research that once required days in the stacks or periodical rooms of libraries can now be done in minutes. A few Google searches, some quick clicks on hyperlinks, and I've got the telltale fact or pithy quote I was after.
>
> (Carr, 2008)

Whether Carr's hypothesis that being able to instantly locate a nugget of information reduces the longer term development of our intelligence is correct is a debatable point and not without its critics. Lehrer (2010) does not disagree with Carr that our lives are becoming a constant stream of interruptions from the computer screen as messages and notifications ping at us from a variety of sources, but argues this might not be such a bad thing. Citing research from the University of California, Lehrer claims that having to quickly analyse and process large amounts of information through the interrogation of internet search engines actually stimulates brain activity and could be seen as making us smarter. This is a debate that will continue for many years and, whatever the outcome, it seems unlikely that we will return to a previous age where research required days spent in libraries poring over books. The internet and whatever succeeds it offer faster access to more information than could ever be found in a single library collection of printed materials and the challenge for information professionals and educators is to help students and users make the best use of them.

This challenge has led to the development of research into helping people, particularly students, with their information literacy skills. Anyone can type a search request into Google and click on the results but being able to decipher those results and make a reasoned judgement on what is appearing on the screen requires critical skills not always apparent amongst students at schools and universities around the world. According to the American Library Association (ALA):

> To be information literate, a person must be able to recognize when information is needed and have the ability to locate, evaluate, and use effectively the needed information.   (ALA, 1989)

The ALA definition of information literacy extends the parameters beyond simply decoding search results and incorporates the ability for users to know which situations require information and then what to do with it once the right information has been found. The ALA's UK equivalent, CILIP, produced a similar definition of information literacy in 2004 where the subject has become a priority area for the professional body:

> Information literacy is knowing when and why you need information, where to find it, and how to evaluate, use and communicate it in an ethical manner.
>   (CILIP, 2004)

CILIP's definition builds on that proposed by the ALA by introducing the notion that information literate people should have an understanding of why the information is required and be able to communicate the findings in an ethical manner. In a practical sense one of the challenges that educators and librarians face is persuading students and users that there are other research resources besides Google and that any information found needs to be critically evaluated for its relevance and provenance. As anyone who has attempted to do this will testify, it is not always an easy task. One of the leading bodies in the UK that has looked at the issues of information literacy and how to address it within the context of higher education is the Society of College, National and University Libraries (SCONUL). In 1999, SCONUL introduced the concept of the Seven Pillars of Information Literacy, which has since been taken up by educators and librarians around the world (SCONUL, 1999). Acknowledging how the digital landscape has changed how students look for, access and use information, SCONUL updated and extended its Seven Pillars model in 2011 although the basic principles of the original model still apply. One of the driving factors behind SCONUL's work in this area has been the recognition that information handling skills are different from skills in using information technology. This has often been an area of confusion for policy makers who have often equated an ability to use a personal computer and associated software with being information literate. SCONUL, drawing on research by Corrall (1998) and others, has disassembled these processes to show the context within which the tools such as computers fit in the broader information landscape. As all of us, not just students, increasingly access and consume information through digital devices, the understanding of how we make sense of this information through research by organizations such as SCONUL will become more important. Educators, information professionals and policy makers need to be able to see beyond the devices and help users evaluate the information that flows through them. This task may become more complex as the services we use online develop and begin to deliver results and information tailored to our previous behaviour. In a similar way that Amazon gives us recommendations based on items we have already purchased, so too Google is presenting search results based on what we have previously searched for and sites we have visited. This means that identical searches performed by different people on different machines may produce differing results. Google is making decisions about the information it thinks is relevant to us as individuals rather than simply responding to a search request. In theory, this is an attractive proposition as our information needs are often based on the context in which we are looking for that information. If Google can better understand that context then we are likely to be served more relevant results. However, not everyone is enthusiastic about this and other similar developments across the plethora of internet-based information services. Pariser believes such developments can be limiting and refers to the phenomenon as the 'filter bubble'. One of his criticisms centres on the importance of being exposed to a variety of information sources and opinions rather than simply those we are comfortable with:

> Consuming information that conforms to our ideas of the world is easy and
> pleasurable; consuming information that challenges us to think in new ways or
> question our assumptions is frustrating and difficult.   (Pariser, 2011)

There is a danger that users of these information services will be unaware of
the filtering that is taking place and assume that the information they are
being presented with is representative of the broader universe of data that
exists on the open web. So rather than simply showing users how to perform
better searches, a role for many information professionals will be to help
information seekers better understand what is going on in the backend
systems of Google, Facebook, Amazon and other internet services.

Information overload

In the space of approximately 20 years most developed economies have
moved from an era of relative information scarcity to one of abundance and,
some would say, overload. Three hundred years ago most of the information
that people processed was sensory information related to their surroundings
and the people they interacted with. As reading skills improved and books
and newspapers became more widely available, new forms of information
were assimilated into the daily lives of individuals. Radio and television in
the 20th century added to this so that by the 1990s most households consumed
a variety of printed and broadcast content with many white collar workers
also processing information via PCs. As we have seen over this and previous
chapters, the internet and its associated services and devices have added a
new layer on top of those analogue sources, with mobile networks providing
access almost wherever we are. Measuring how much information exists is
an almost impossible task as assumptions need to be made about what is
being measured. For example, estimating the storage required to digitally
store a book requires decisions to be made about whether the digital copy
would be a scanned, facsimile copy or simply a reduction of the contents into
an Ascii file that would be considerable smaller. However, attempts have been
made and, despite issues around accuracy, show that the information
available to us in a variety of formats has grown faster than most commentators imagined. In 1997, Lesk (1997) estimated that there existed several
thousand petabytes (1000 terabytes) of information globally and in 2000
Lyman and Varian (2000) calculated the world was producing between one
and two exabytes (1000 petabytes) of unique information annually. By 2015,
.internet switch manufacturer Cisco estimates that the amount of information
flowing across the internet globally will be 966 exabytes, much of which will
be the data that flows across our computer and mobile phone screens (Cisco,

2011). To put that into perspective, 966 exabytes is the equivalent of approximately 1800 trillion books or the contents of 96 million US Libraries of Congress. Clearly, a lot of this information sits on computer servers and is never presented to humans for processing by our limited intellects and attention spans, but a significant proportion goes into the e-mails, web pages, RSS feeds, Facebook updates and tweets that are constantly pinging at us from our phones and computers at home and work. Market research company, Radicati estimates that an average of 294 billion e-mails were sent every day in 2010, approximately 43 e-mails each day for every person on the planet (Radicati Group, 2010). Coping with this tsunami of data is becoming a burden for many of us and a variety of tools and methodologies have emerged to try and wrest back control. Hemp (2009) points out that office workers spend an average of two hours a day dealing with e-mail and argues that this is having a negative effect on productivity at work. Part of the problem, he believes, is workers themselves who perpetuate the e-mail problem by sending out too many unnecessary messages to fellow workers. As well as helping workers process e-mails more efficiently, a solution Hemp (2009) suggests is to 'encourage them to be more selective and intelligent about creating and distributing information in the first place'.

Perhaps one of the most widely used systems for coping with the digital age is the Getting Things Done (GTD) methodology developed in the USA by David Allen (2002). At the core of Allen's GTD system is the acknowledgement that the human brain is excellent at innovative and creative thinking but poor at storing and recalling information. Relying on our brains and not a trusted system to store information, according to Allen, causes us stress through the worry that we will forget things that need to be done. His solution is to create a system, paper or computer-based, that will act as the storage system for our to do lists and project files, freeing our minds to engage in more creative thinking and finding solutions to issues at home and work. The plethora of software that claims to be GTD-compliant, the GTD training courses that take place around the world and the hundreds of thousands of copies of Allen's book that have been sold indicate there is significant demand for a solution to coping with information overload.

Implications for information professionals

Just as mobile phones allowed users to make calls away from their homes and desks, changing the way we think about communications, so too is mobile broadband impacting on the distribution of information. The ability to access and transmit information while on the go is changing how many information workers operate and creating new industries in the process. As information access is untethered from physical spaces, the impact on libraries, already affected by the rise of the fixed internet, may become more pronounced. Mobile communication technologies make the possibility of information being available anytime, anywhere, to anyone closer than ever, and institutions operating within the scarcity model of information provision and expecting users to visit their premises may become less relevant. On the surface this may appear to be bad news for the traditional library, particularly public ones. However, the wireless revolution may also present opportunities as mobile workers look for new places to work. Cassavoy (2011) quotes a freelance worker who prefers to work out of coffee houses in the Austin, Texas, area: 'I am the type of person who would go crazy without being around other people. Working from home or a rented office would get lonely fast.'

A frequent discussion amongst library professionals in recent years has been whether libraries should change their configuration to appeal to a broader range of users. Within academic libraries this has resulted in areas set aside for group working, social meetings and the serving of refreshments. Waxman et al. (2007) discuss their research into what students want from libraries and conclude that the creation of more convivial surroundings including the introduction of coffee bars can encourage more students into university libraries. Others are less convinced by such developments, particularly when it applies to public libraries. Clee (2005) acknowledges that libraries need to change to remain relevant in the 21st century but fears that some libraries 'appear to have settled for becoming community information points with coffee shops attached'. Whether appealing to coffee addicts is the right strategic move for libraries is debatable, but offering a working environment such as that favoured by Cassavoy's mobile worker above may be sensible for some.

Information professionals are certainly at the forefront of experimenting with many of the new mobile information services. Location-based services such as Foursquare, Google Latitude and Facebook Places allows mobile users to share their location with friends as well as the owners of the places they visit. Users can see where their friends are and what places they have visited, while location owners can offer special offers to those 'checking in' to their location. While there are obvious marketing applications to such services as well as privacy implications, many libraries have also been experimenting with them. Cuddy and Glassman (2010) describe the use of location-based services by libraries in the USA and point out that the services can be useful for notifying visitors about events at the library as well as practical information such as opening hours and upcoming workshops. Rethlefsen (2010) believes that, privacy issues aside, these services can encourage more people to visit a library as the social element of checking in can appeal to younger users. Location-based services are still at an early stage of development and have not met with the initial success that many had anticipated. A browse through public and academic libraries in the UK and USA that had a presence on Foursquare in late 2011 revealed a large number of institutions using the service. One of the most popular was Bobst Library at New York University, which had amassed just over 12,000 check-ins from 2355 people in the two years it had been on the service.

Concluding comments

In this chapter we have seen how the rise of computing devices, deskbound and portable, and the information ecosystems that surround them are changing the ways we consume information. For publishers, information professionals and end-users these changes present opportunities for improving the way we work and are entertained. However, they also lead to challenges as we attempt to cope with the interruptions that these devices bring and the sheer quantity of content that needs to be processed and made sense of. While we are still coming to terms with this brave new digital world it is inevitable that solutions to educating users in information literacy and systems for dealing with information overload will be found and adopted. Perhaps more interesting are the implications for information production. In Chapter 2 we saw how new technologies are leading to new models of information production and, in some ways, we have come full circle. As social media and interactive publishing platforms such as blogs encourage readers to add their own thoughts and comments, so a new layer of richness is added to the original content. The story does not necessarily end as the journalist's work goes to the printing presses but lives on as readers post their views to the web either directly to the newspaper's website or indirectly via platforms such as Facebook or Twitter. For information professionals this increases the sources they need to keep track of as the boundaries of the reference world move beyond the journal and the online database.

QUESTIONS TO THINK ABOUT

1. What are the key factors which determine the success of a mobile computing device?
2. Will printed books still exist in 2020?
3. What is the role of a library in a world of e-books?
4. Does having access to information wherever we are make us better workers?

CHAPTER 6
Conclusion

Introduction

We've seen in the preceding chapters how the digitization of information is transforming a number of industries including book, newspaper and music publishing, as well as changing the roles and responsibilities of those who manage information within organizations. While there is a danger for industry commentators and analysts to overplay the role of technology in influencing organizational and societal change, an objective of this book has been to show that real changes are under way. Examples and case studies have been used to illustrate how established organizations are responding to these challenges and how new companies are being formed to take advantage of them. Alongside the focus on organizational change has been a consideration of the impact these developments are having more broadly on the work of information professionals. This concluding chapter will bring together some of the themes and issues already discussed and examine what they might mean for information workers, publishers and, more broadly, society in the second decade of the 21st century.

Implications for information professionals

It seems strange that at a time when the wealth of developed economies is increasingly dependent on information industries, the jobs of many information professionals are under increasing pressure and, in some sectors, under threat. Cuts to public libraries in the USA and UK since the credit crunch of 2008 have been widely reported and academic and school libraries have also been under financial pressures to do more with less. Why are the professionals trained to manage information not reaping the benefits of the information revolution? A major reason is the move from analogue information artefacts such as books, newspapers and journals to digitized formats that have required new technical skills not traditionally taught on the academic courses accredited by professional bodies such as CILIP and the ALA. Another factor has been the mass adoption of internet access in households as well as the accessibility of cheap computing devices. These developments have allowed many people to find the information they need at home rather than calling on the services of libraries and information professionals. However, as we have seen in the preceding chapters the rise of new models of information production, distribution and consumption has also offered opportunities for information professionals to capitalize on their skills.

The knowledge management opportunity

Some readers will remember the knowledge management boom of the 1990s when every technology vendor from IBM to Microsoft was claiming how their systems would allow companies to capture the collective knowledge of their employees. Tapping in to these knowledge bases, it was claimed, would give a company a competitive advantage over its competitors, as knowledge replaced capital as the way to dominate a market. Researchers and analysts such as Davenport and Prusak (1998) and Nonaka and Takeuchi (1995) presented compelling cases for the ability of organizations to capture, store and make accessible their employee's knowledge for use in the creation of new products and services and to improve the efficiency of business processes. For many information professionals at the time it seemed an opportunity to move into roles more closely aligned with their employers' core business and the not insignificant chance to increase their salaries. However, the initial promise of many knowledge management tools and techniques was never realized and the phrase took on rather negative connotations often associated with the dot com bust of the early 2000s. Tom Wilson's (2002) article, 'The Nonsense of Knowledge Management', exposed many of the unsupportable claims made by knowledge management advocates and extended the debate on whether knowledge is actually manageable. While the term fell out of favour with many information professionals for a number of years at the beginning of this century, there has been something of a resurgence more recently. Just as the rise of Web 2.0 tools and technologies such as blogs, wikis, social media and RSS have helped rejuvenate the technology sector, so too have they raised hopes that this time the technology might be able to deliver on earlier promises. An easy to deploy and cheap tool such as a wiki allows organizations to easily share information between employees and, while it is debatable if this could be called knowledge sharing, it certainly provides a platform for a collective repository of useful information. Levy (2009) and Lee and Lan (2007) have shown how the collaborative nature of many Web 2.0 tools lends itself to the principles of knowledge sharing and that many of the modern tools are more user-friendly than the systems of the 1990s. Davidson (2011) argues that the power of these tools to help organizations better share knowledge aligns well with the core competences of many information professionals and presents opportunities for them to apply their skills in this new environment. One of the advantages of modern tools such as wikis and other collaborative platforms is that many of them are easy to experiment with outside the workplace, allowing users to become comfortable with them before making the case to managers for a more formal roll-out. Solutions that are hosted outside the organization and in the provider's 'cloud' may require less assistance from IT support staff, making deployment less expensive and demanding on internal resources.

The future of search

We know that Google has changed the way most of us look for information to the extent that the verb 'to Google' someone or something is now commonly used. It was Google's use of counting links between web pages as a key factor in determining results that set it apart from other search engines and has given it a near monopoly in internet search. The implications of this for information professionals has already been discussed but it is worth considering how people's searching habits may change in the future.

One of the complaints often levelled against search engines such as Google is that they only present users with links to web pages that the provider thinks are relevant. It is still up to the searcher to click on those links and find the information on the resulting pages. Lau (2011) describes how Yahoo!, utilizing the technology of Microsoft's search engine, Bing, is positioning itself as a provider of answers rather than links. Although Lau says this will not happen before 2014, the ambition is for users to be presented with an answer to their question rather than a page of links. In some respects this is similar to the Wolfram Alpha web service, which calls itself an answer-engine. Launched in 2009, it draws on structured data sets from a variety of sources to provide precise answers to questions such as 'will it rain tomorrow', which produces tables of local weather forecast data and the percentage chance that it will rain tomorrow. The company claims that its answer-engine draws on over 10 trillion pieces of data from primary sources and utilizes more than 50,000 types of algorithms and equations to manipulate the data when responding to queries. While it is efficient at providing answers to questions which have unambiguous answers it is far less useful in helping choose a new camera or book a holiday where judgement becomes a factor. However, for some of the questions that a typical public library reference desk receives, the service certainly can be a viable substitute. An interesting development in late 2011 was the launch of the Siri voice recognition service that was built into the iOS 5 Apple operating system. This allows users to interact with their iPhones and iPads via voice commands and questions. Of note is that Siri utilizes Wolfram Alpha for questions that a user might want answers to. While Siri was launched as a beta service and, if it succeeds, will take several years to evolve into a tool used by the masses, it does indicate a direction of travel for aspects of the search market. By combining the natural language capabilities of Siri and its ability to make sense of spoken commands and questions with computational services such as Wolfram Alpha, it is possible to envisage a future where talking to our machines and asking them questions will be commonplace. Arthur (2011) describes how the mouse transformed how we interacted with computers in the 1980s and posits that if we can get over inhibitions of talking to computers then Siri may be just as revolutionary.

Ninja librarians

We saw in Chapter 2 how social media services such as Facebook and Twitter are producing new forms of information that are becoming a valuable data resource for researchers and marketers. Other groups interested in mining this data are the security services that monitor the social networks to gain insights into the activities of individuals and organizations they have an 'interest in'. Hill (2011) describes how a CIA office in the USA employs several hundred analysts who describe themselves as ninja librarians to track the social media sphere. While security services around the world have been monitoring electronic communications for many years, it is only recently that they have been able to eavesdrop on the open communications that take place across social media services. Hill (2011) points out that the 'ninja librarians' were able to track and predict developments in the Arab uprisings of 2011 by looking in aggregate at the tweets and Facebook postings of those involved and observing events on the street. Although these analysts are not librarians in the traditional sense of the word, it is interesting that they have co-opted the term to describe their activities and, perhaps, indicates an evolution of the description for people who work with information.

Not many organizations have the resources of the CIA to employ hundreds of people to monitor traffic on social networks but an increasing number would like to have that capability. One of the approaches to allow this has been the development of sentiment analysis, which uses computer algorithms to infer meaning from digital text. While any search engine can create an index of web pages based on the words it finds, their proximity to other words and its interpretation of the main keywords, none of them can yet effectively and accurately determine what it means in a human sense of understanding. Artificial intelligence systems and natural language processing research has made significant inroads in this area but human language and its textual representation are still too nuanced for computers to fully understand what the author is saying. However, services do exist which claim to be able to offer an interpretation of the sentiment of digital messages, especially social media content. These are of particular interest to companies wishing to monitor their reputations online across a range of websites, discussion forums and social media. By receiving an early warning that negative discussions and comments might be emerging online, a company can evaluate what can be done to address those issues such as responding to adverse comments or putting right problems with its products or services. British software company Autonomy offers a service called IDOL which it claims:

> helps not only to protect the company's brand and reputation but actually influences strategic investment in the product and reduces costs. Reputation analysis is also legally attestable and can support litigation where unfounded, defamatory comments made by rogue journalists or competitors negatively influence the company's reputation.
>
> (Autonomy, 2011)

Such a product is similar to press cutting services utilized by organizations for many years to track what is being said about them and their competitors, but allows humans to be removed from the equation. A traditional press cutting service, even when the collection stage is automated, requires people to read the news stories and interpret what they mean for the client and, crucially, whether it is positive or negative reporting. A service such as Autonomy's IDOL can present the client with a summary of what is being written across a range of online sources and interpret the meaning. Following an exhaustive and detailed analysis of a number of sentiment analysis technologies, Pang and Lee (2008) conclude that although there is still much work to be done in improving the accuracy of the underlying technologies, it is possible for organizations to obtain reasonably accurate and useful results. The logical conclusion of developments in natural language processing and sentiment analysis tools is the removal of the need for people like the CIA's ninja librarians whose judgement is currently relied on to interpret the disparate streams of information flowing across the internet. Just as the search engine has undermined the perceived value of the library reference desk perhaps Siri, Wolfram Alpha and IDOL will remove the need for the information professionals and analysts who make sense of the information once it has been retrieved.

By this stage, if you are a librarian, library student or another kind of information professional, you might be thinking of throwing in the towel and considering another line of work or study. However, if that is the case then think again as while new technologies undoubtedly make some tasks and roles obsolete, they also create new ones. In the spirit of adding the 2.0 suffix to new ways of working, MIT academic Andrew McAfee coined the phrase Enterprise 2.0 to describe the changes taking place in the ways that organizations are restructuring to take advantage of new computing technologies (McAfee, 2009). As an explanation for the key processes underlying the evolution of Enterprise 2.0 McAfee created the acronym SLATES, which stands for Search, Links, Authorship, Tags, Extensions, Signalling. At its core, SLATES describes the processes by which information is produced, classified, distributed and then found by employees and utilizes a range of modern technologies such as blogs, wikis, RSS and other tools that facilitate information creation and exchange. What immediately should stand out to any information professionals is that these are the very tools and processes that are at the heart of much information work: classifying information, sharing it and helping others to find the data they need. If McAfee is correct that successful enterprises of the future will need to focus on developing these areas and competences, then perhaps the outlook for information professionals is bright.

Implications for publishers

In previous chapters we have seen how new technologies of information production and distribution are transforming the publishing industry across a range of media types. Cheap computing devices and the internet have lowered the barriers to entry for anyone who wants to build a publishing empire. For some established companies this challenge is proving particularly difficult to overcome and newspaper publishers in particular are seeing reduced sales and profits. While new content creation companies such as TWiT and the Huffington Post described in Chapter 2 are making inroads into the media landscape it should be noted that traditional publishers are not all sitting on their hands. They recognize that change is inevitable and that their business models will have to adapt to the digital media landscape. Hyams (2011b) argues that in their attempts to make this change publishers are becoming technology providers by developing platforms more friendly to digital distribution and consumption through computing devices. This, she points out, is particularly the case amongst academic publishers, who are formatting their content for use on e-book readers and developing new purchasing models, including the rental of e-textbooks. While renting a key text may be cheaper for students it also, according to Hyams, cuts out the resale of second-hand books for which publishers receive no income. As these new models and technologies evolve it is inevitable that some will fall by the way and others will become established practice. Whether they will continue to generate similar profits for publishers, as the traditional models of book and journal publishing have done in the past, remains to be seen. A large driver of success will be the extent to which they fit with the consumption habits of digital consumers who increasingly expect to find the information they need when they want it and in a format that is convenient.

The copyright challenge

One of the reasons that many publishers have been slow to adapt to the digital landscape is the fear of piracy. As we saw in Chapter 4, the music industry is still struggling to develop new business models that can cope with the rise of illegal music downloads via websites such as The Pirate Bay. Although there are rigorous debates over the extent to which piracy has been directly responsible for the travails of the music industry, it is undeniable that digitized content is far more easily copied and distributed than analogue formats. The deployment by publishers of DRM software that restricts what consumers can do with content in terms of sharing and copying has been one response to this problem. The rise of streaming media services whereby consumers pay a fixed monthly fee for access to music, which ceases when the subscription ends, is another response. What links these attempts to enforce intellectual property rights in a digital world is a belief among the content owners that existing copyright laws must be maintained and that the new technologies must fit within that legal framework. An alternative approach has been to question whether our ideas on the ownership of ideas and content need to adapt to the new models of information production, distribution and consumption. In Chapter 5 the example was given of how an e-book version of an out-of-copyright text, *Alice's Adventures in Wonderland*, had been locked down with DRM to the extent that, under the terms of the licence, the book could not be shared, given away or read aloud. The source of that example was a Professor of Law at Harvard University, Lawrence Lessig. His criticisms of copyright legislation in the USA and other developed economies led, with the help of others, to the creation of an initiative known as Creative Commons, a non-profit organization which offers licences to content creators outlining how their works can be re-used. Creative Commons licences are not designed to replace the ownership rights inferred by copyright legislation but to offer a more flexible approach for the re-use of original content, whether music, writing, videos or images. Content owners can choose from a variety of licences that range from only allowing their creations to be used for non-commercial uses to the free re-use for any purpose, including commercial re-use provided that author attribution is made. In 2009, eight years after its launch, the organization estimated that over 350 million works had been licensed under the Creative Commons system (http://creativecommons.org/ about/history). In the broader picture of the creative industries this is a relatively small number and the licences have been used largely by smaller, independent artists and authors but the Creative Commons ideals are significant because they offer a new way of thinking about intellectual property. Just as open source software projects are transforming, albeit rather slowly, important segments of the technology industry, so the Creative Commons initiative and whatever follows it are creating a grassroots movement of change amongst content creators. In 2009 Wikipedia, one of the world's most visited websites, adopted a Creative Commons licence for all the content it hosts. In the networked and interconnected world of information we are now entering the old models of locked-down content that suited the analogue production and distribution models look less sustainable.

Publishing for an algorithm

In early 2011, Google made some important changes to its algorithm that decides which order to rank search results. The update, known as Panda, was an attempt to counter the rise of online publishers whose business model was to create content that would rank highly in Google search results and make money for the publishers through online advertising. These publishers, often referred to as content farms, typically produced low-quality outputs written by freelancers for very little money. Articles were commissioned on the basis of search terms being used by searchers and then optimized for high ranking by Google by filling them with keywords and phrases that would be picked up when Google indexed their pages. Over the preceding months Google users had been increasingly unhappy with their search results, which tended to be dominated by a number of content farm sites and were perceived by many to be of low quality and not providing the information they wanted. As any search engine lives and dies by the quality of the results it serves to users, Google realized it had to act to restore its reputation. The impact of Panda and subsequent updates to its algorithm has been significant, with Anderson (2011) claiming that 12% of search results have been affected and that the impact has largely been felt by the publishing companies generally perceived to be producing the low-quality content. No doubt such companies will try to find new ways to get round the revised algorithm and the battle will continue. However, what is more significant about these developments is what it says about publishing in an online world dominated by a single company. With two-thirds of all internet searches in the USA going through Google and this figure rising to 90% in much of Europe, the company is a gatekeeper to much online content. It is not surprising that under such a regime some publishers will adapt their business models and outputs to fit with the way that Google works. In a pre-internet world it would be similar to most people only being able to shop in one bookshop that had very strict rules about which books it would stock. Publishers would have to produce books that fitted with those rules or risk losing their channel to customers. As Google itself moves into the content business via YouTube, Google Books and Google Music this has the potential to distort the publishing business and the company will face increasing legislative scrutiny in much the same way that Microsoft did in the 1990s. Diversity in publishing is essential and it would be ironic if a company that revolutionized how we find information was ultimately responsible for reducing the sources that it is able to index.

Hooked on tablets

We saw in Chapter 5 how new portable computing devices are changing the ways many of use consume information, in particular news. Research in the USA showed that in mid-2011, 11% of adults owned a tablet computing device and more than half of them used it daily to read the news (Mitchell, Christian and Rosenstiel, 2011). These findings are significant because of the numbers they represent but also because they come less than two years after the launch of the first tablet device, the Apple iPad. The research also discovered that 77% of tablet owners use them every day for an average of 90 minutes. As new entrants to the tablet market emerge and the prices of devices comes down, it seems likely that they will become more widely used and could become the dominant platform via which news content is consumed. Many newspaper and magazine publishers see the tablet as a potential saviour in the light of falling circulations and advertising revenues from their print operations. Some publishers have developed apps for the presentation of their content, for example, *The Economist* app offers a reading experience similar to the printed magazine.

Another approach has been the development of apps such as Pulse, Flipboard and Livestand, which aggregate content from a variety of publishers and present it as a form of news stand where users can pick and choose which sources to read. Some of these services also integrate social media streams and RSS feeds to create a mashup of sources from traditional and online-only publishers. Part of the appeal of apps like Flipboard that offer this functionality is the clean interface they offer users rather than the more cluttered and confusing presentation of RSS readers, which have never had mass appeal. However, the challenge for publishers will be finding ways to generate revenue from presenting their content in tablet-friendly ways. While this has proved very difficult, and impossible for some, on the open web it is hoped that consumers will be willing to pay for content if presented in a user-friendly way. With tablets this challenge may be easier for publishers as the mechanisms for handling payments are already in place. Apple, a key producer of tablet devices, already handles payments from millions of consumers via its iTunes service. Google, the company behind the Android Marketplace, also handles financial transactions for app sales, and a new entrant to the tablet market, Amazon, is the world's largest online retailer. While the mechanisms for taking payments are in place, concerns amongst publishers may develop into a fear that some or all of the three companies just mentioned will become monopolistic gatekeepers to consumers in the same way that many music publishers feel Apple has done with iTunes and music sales. However, in the short term at least, publishers probably have little choice but to adapt to the world of tablets.

Implications for society

Throughout this book we have seen how the new models of information production, distribution and consumption are changing the ways publishers manage their operations and information professionals deal with the new types and formats of information that their users require. However, it should be remembered that many of these changes are having broader impacts on society at large. When most people come to rely on the internet as the primary platform for finding and consuming information then any changes to the way that platform operates will have consequences for all of us. We saw this in Chapter 4 with the issue of net neutrality and the threats to the relative openness of the internet posed by competing commercial interests. As technology becomes more embedded into our work and social lives, the decisions of regulators, politicians and companies such as Google and Apple can shape the trajectories of innovation and development of the networks and devices we rely on.

Internet everywhere

The endpoints of the internet are generally the web servers that hold the content and the devices via which we access that content. For the consumption of information by individuals this has worked very well, but imagine a future where inanimate devices such as your fridge, car or even a can of baked beans can send information over the network. At a basic level this already occurs in many libraries with the automatic checking in and out of books via the RFID technology embedded in chips inside books. Tales of intelligent fridges that can automatically order food for you when they detect the milk or eggs are running out have been circulating since the internet became a fixture in households. However, the rise of low-cost computer chips, mobile internet connections and the deployment of virtually unlimited IP addresses via IPv6 are making this a more realistic possibility. According to Miller and Bilton (2011), Google is one of the companies that is investing millions of dollars in researching the development of such smart devices via its secret laboratory known as Google X. Some of the household items that could be connected via what is commonly called the 'internet of things' are:

> a garden planter (so it could be watered from afar); a coffee pot (so it could be set to brew remotely); or a light bulb (so it could be turned off remotely)
>
> (Miller and Bilton, 2011)

Although the examples described above are relatively trivial the implications of such a development are significant, particularly for businesses that are keen to streamline their processes such as stock and inventory control. If a warehouse or factory can automatically order stock items as they run low, it could transform the manufacturing process and reduce inefficiencies and waste. Chui, Löffler and Roberts (2010) imagine a not-too distant future where pills can be ingested and send back images of the body they are passing through to help with medical diagnoses, and billboards will scan pedestrians and show advertisements they consider appropriate for the audience. The extent to which the internet does become embedded in the everyday items all around us remains to be seen but it is inevitable that where a business case can be made for it then companies will be keen to exploit the potential of the internet of things. One of the results of this will be a massive increase in the amount of data flowing through the internet as billions of items are sending out signals to remote listening posts.

Nowhere to hide

Another issue to be considered if the internet of things becomes a reality is the impact on personal privacy. While our local supermarket might like to know our fridge is running low on milk and needs to order some more, we might not be so comfortable giving up this information. When the internet is everywhere how much autonomy will we retain when our devices are taking control of our lives? This is already becoming an issue with location-aware smartphones and some of the services that take advantage of this capability. Apps such as Google Latitude and Foursquare generate data that is a marketer's dream, with information about our preference for cafés, shops and hotels being sent out to a range of companies, sometimes without our knowledge. Alongside the data we share across social networks and via search engines, some of the larger internet companies are building up detailed profiles of our friends, where we work, what we like and where we go.

As the largest social network, Facebook and its more than 800 million users is a prime target for privacy campaigners. The company has probably not helped itself in this respect with its frequent and sometimes confusing changes to the default privacy settings it ascribes to users. A starting point for many organizations that need to screen job applicants is the social web, where online profiles can tell a potential employer whether or not to send out an invitation for interview. Services such as Klout that apply numerical scores to the social media profiles of individuals based on their activity and who they are connected to are taking this to the next level. Just as web pages rely on the Google Pagerank algorithm for their visibility in search results, so too might we be judged in the future by our social media score, which will determine where we study and who will employ us. When decisions are increasingly made by computers, and computers work best with unambiguous, numerical data, then perhaps our worth will be decided by an algorithm.

Concluding comments

The breadth of subjects and issues covered in a book of this length have inevitably resulted in a broad overview and discussion of some of the new models of information production, distribution and consumption. The intention has been to introduce readers to some of the key technologies that are changing the ways information is created and found and the implications these changes have for information professionals, publishers and society. We are seeing a restructuring of the information industries with many publishers becoming technology companies and technology giants such as Google encroaching on the territory of a range of content producers. Just as the invention of the printing press over 500 years ago helped usher in the Age of Enlightenment, which radically changed how we looked at our world, so too may the new digital technologies of content production and distribution transform the world in the 21st century. Brooke (2011) certainly shares this view and is optimistic that digital technologies can have a benevolent impact on society: 'Technology is breaking down traditional social barriers of status, class, power, wealth and geography, replacing them with an ethos of collaboration and transparency.' Perhaps an age where information is everywhere and accessible to everyone will help us overcome some of the challenges the planet faces as global warming and economic and political uncertainties require new ideas and ways of thinking. Whether the emerging models of information production, distribution and consumption are moving societies towards such an age of openness remains to be seen. There are powerful interests, political and economic, that would like to use the digital revolution to extend their control over markets and citizens. In this respect, many of the emerging technologies present a double-edged sword: Google and Facebook may know more about us than we would like, but equally they provide a window to a wealth of information resources that can help us make better and more informed decisions.

References

Abram, S. (2007) The Future of Reference in Special Libraries Is What Information Pros Can Make It, *Information Outlook*, October, 35.

ALA (1989) *Presidential Committee on Information Literacy: final report*, American Library Association, www.ala.org/ala/mgrps/divs/acrl/publications/whitepapers/presidential.cfm.

Allen, D. (2002) *Getting Things Done: how to achieve stress-free productivity*, Piatkus Books.

Al-Nakaash, P. (2011) *The Future of Content Aggregation*, LexisNexis White Paper, www.lexisnexis.co.uk/media/insights/The-Future-of-content-Aggregation.pdf.

Alpert, J. and Hajaj, N. (2008) *We Know the Web Was Big...*, http://googleblog.blogspot.com/2008/07/we-knew-web-was-big.html.

Amazon (2011) *Amazon.co.uk Kindle License Agreement and Terms of Use*, www.amazon.co.uk/gp/help/customer/display.html?nodeId=200501450.

Anderson, M. (2011) *How Google Panda and Places Updates Created a Rollercoaster Ride for IYP Traffic*, http://searchengineland.com/how-google-panda-places-updates-created-a-rollercoaster-ride-for-iyp-traffic-101683.

Arthur, C. (2011) Voice Recognition: has it come of age?, *Guardian*, www.guardian.co.uk/technology/2011/nov/20/voice-recognition-apple-siri.

Autonomy (2011) *Real-Time Sentiment Analysis*, www.autonomy.com/content/Functionality/idol-functionality-sentiment/index.en.html.

Babcock, C. (2006) Data, Data, Everywhere, *Information Week*, www.informationweek.com/shared/printableArticle.jhtml;jsessionid=E1BNEBPSPXE1JQE1GHPCKH4ATMY32JVN?articleID=175801775.

Barnett, E. and Alleyne, R. (2011) Self Publishing Writer Becomes Million Seller, *Telegraph*, www.telegraph.co.uk/culture/books/booknews/8589963/Self-publishing-writer-becomes-million-seller.html.

Battelle, J. (2006) *The Search: how Google and its rivals rewrote the rules of business and transformed our culture*, Nicholas Brealey Publishing.

Bell, D. (1973) *The Coming of Post-Industrial Society: a venture in social forecasting*, Basic Books.

Bentley, J. (2011) A Good Search, *Information World Review*, September/October, 14–15.

Betteridge, I. (2004) iPod Market Share Falls to 87%, *PC Magazine*, www.pcmag.com/article2/0,2817,1712062,00.asp#fbid=irDZQ7jrChJ.

Bhattacharjee, S. (2010) *The Business Intelligence Market Outlook*, Business Insights.

Bintliff, E. (2011) Emap Boosted by Online Intelligence, *Financial Times*, www.ft.com/cms/s/0/d8dcaf2a-2ca8-11e0-83bd-00144feab49a.html.

British Library (2011) *The British Library and Google to Make 250,000 Books Available to All*, http://pressandpolicy.bl.uk/Press-Releases/The-British-Library-and-Google-to-make-250-000-books-available-to-all-4fc.aspx.

Broady-Preston, J. And Felice, J. (2006) Customers, Relationships and Libraries: University of Malta – a case study, *Aslib Proceedings*, **58** (6), 525–36.

Brooke, H. (2011) *The Revolution Will Be Digitised: dispatches from the information war*, William Heinemann.

Budnarowska, C. and Marciniak, R. (2009) How Do Fashion Retail Customers Search on the Internet?: exploring the use of data mining tools to enhance CRM, *15th Conference of the European Association for Education and Research in Commercial Distribution (EAERCD) held on 15–17 July 2009, University of Surrey*, (unpublished).

Bughin, J., Chui, M. and Manyika, J. (2010) Clouds, Big Data, and Smart Assets: ten tech-enabled business trends to watch, *McKinsey Quarterly*, Issue 4, 26–43.

Burley, D. (2011) To 'Appify' Old Media, We Need a New Approach, http://gigaom.com/2011/01/17/to-appify-old-media-we-need-a-new-approac.

Cane, A. (2009) The Final Frontier of Business Advantage, *Financial Times*, (27 November), 2–3.

Carr, N. (2008) Is Google Making Us Stupid? What the internet is doing to our brains, *The Atlantic*, **301** (6), 56–63.

Carr, N. (2010) *The Shallows*, Atlantic Books.

Carroll, E. and Romano, J. (2010) *Your Digital Afterlife: when Facebook, Flickr and Twitter are your estate, what's your legacy?*, New Riders.

Cassavoy, L. (2011) *Starbucks Is My Office: a guide for mobile over-caffeinated workers*, www.pcworld.com/businesscenter/article/225471/starbucks_is_my_office_a_guide_for_mobile_overcaffeinated_workers.html.

CFoI (1998) *Lord Chancellor Presents 1997 Freedom of Information Awards*, Campaign for Freedom of Information, www.cfoi.org.uk/awards97pr.html.

Chen, C. and Chen, A. (2007) Using Data Mining Technology to Provide a Recommendation Service in the Digital Library, *The Electronic Library*, **25** (6), 711–24.

Chui, M., Löffler, M. and Roberts, R. (2010) The Internet of Things, *McKinsey Quarterly*, Issue 2, 70–9.

CILIP (2004) *Information Literacy: definition*, Chartered Institute of Library and Information Professionals, www.cilip.org.uk/get-involved/advocacy/information-literacy/Pages/definition.aspx.

Cisco (2011) *Cisco Visual Networking Index: forecast and methodology, 2010–2015*, www.cisco.com/en/US/solutions/collateral/ns341/ns525/ns537/ns705/ns827/white_paper_c11-481360.pdf.

Clarke, R. (2000) *Information Wants to be Free...*, www.rogerclarke.com/II/IWtbF.html.

Clee, N. (2005) The Book Business, *New Statesman*, www.newstatesman.com/200507180047.

COI (2009) *Engaging Through Social Media*, Central Office of Information, http://coi.gov.uk/documents/Engaging_through_social_media.pdf.

COI (2010) *Reporting on Progress: central government websites*, Central Office of Information, http://coi.gov.uk/websitemetricsdata/websitemetrics2009-10.pdf.

Corrall, S. (1998) Key Skills for Students in Higher Education, *SCONUL Newsletter*, Winter, 25–9.

Cross, M. (2007) Public Sector Information 'Worth Billions', *Guardian*, www.guardian.co.uk/technology/2007/nov/15/freeourdata.news.

Cuddy, C. and Glassman, N. (2010) Location-Based Services: Foursquare and Gowalla, should libraries play?, *Journal of Electronic Resources in Medical Libraries*, 7 (4), 336–43.

Davenport, T. and Prusak, L. (1998) *Working Knowledge: how organizations manage what they know*, Harvard Business School Press.

Davenport, T. H., Harris, J. G. and Morison, R. (2010) *Analytics at Work: smarter decisions, better results*, Harvard Business School Press.

Davey, J. (2009) Every Little Bit of Data Helps Tesco Rule Retail, *Sunday Times*, (4 October), 7.

Davidson, C. (2011) *Designing for Flow: part 2 – new opportunity, new role and new tools*, http://futureready365.sla.org/11/01/designing-for-flow-part-2.

Davoudi, S. (2011) UK Slips to Fourth Place in Global Music Sales, *Financial Times*, (28 March), 21.

Dellavalle et al. (2003) Going, Going, Gone: lost Internet references, *Science*, **302** (5646), 787–8.

De Saulles, M. (2011) Social Media and Local Government in England: who is doing what? *Proceedings of the 11th European Conference on E-Government, held on 16–17 June, University of Ljubljana*, Academic Conferences International.

Dishman, L. (2011) Innovation Agents: Jeff Dachis, Founder, Dachis Group, Fast Company, www.fastcompany.com/1716575/innovation-agents-jeff-dachis-founder-dachis-group.

Economist, The (2009) The Internet's Librarian, *The Economist*, **390** (8621), 34.

Economist, The (2010) The Data Deluge, *The Economist*, **394** (8671), 11.

Economist, The (2011) A New, Improved Hit Machine: discovering musical talent, *The Economist*, **401** (8756), 84.

Envisional (2011) *An Estimate of Infringing Use of the Internet*, http://documents.envisional.com/docs/Envisional-Internet_Usage-Jan2011.pdf.

Fehrenbacher, K. (2011) *Cool Finnish Weather the New Hotness for Data Centers*, http://gigaom.com/cleantech/cool-finnish-weather-the-new-hotness-for-green-data-centers.

Fenez, M. and van Der Donk, M. (2010) *From Paper to Platform: transforming the B2B publishing business model, Digital Age*, PricewaterhouseCoopers.

Gabbatt, A. (2011) Amazon and Waterstones Report Downloads Eclipsing Printed Book Sales, *Guardian*, www.guardian.co.uk/books/2011/may/19/amazon-waterstones-ebook-sales.

Gantz, J. and Reinsel, D. (2011) Extracting Value From Chaos, *IDC Iview*, http://idcdocserv.com/1142.

Gibson, A. (2010) *Local By Social: how local authorities can use social media to achieve more for less*, www.idea.gov.uk/idk/aio/17801438.

Giddens, A. (1990) *The Consequences of Modernity*, Cambridge.

Ginsberg, J. et al. (2009) Detecting Influenza Epidemics Using Search Engine Query Data, *Nature*, **457** (7232), 1012–15.

Graham, G. and Hill, J. (2009) The Regional Newspaper Industry Value Chain in the Digital Age, *OR Insight*, **22**, 165–83.

Guardian, The (2010) *British Library Indicates Shift to Digital*, www.guardian.co.uk/government-computing-network/2010/sep/20/british-library-2020-vision-predictions-20sep10.

Hall, K. (2011) Public Data Could Boost the Economy but Whose Information Is It Anyway? *Computer Weekly*, 6 December, 4.

Halliday, J. (2010) ISPs Should Be Free to Abandon Net Neutrality, says Ed Vaizey, *Guardian*, www.guardian.co.uk/technology/2010/nov/17/net-neutrality-ed-vaizey.

Harris, D. (2011) *Apple Launches iCloud; here's what powers it*, http://gigaom.com/cloud/apple-launches-icloud-heres-what-powers-it.

Harris, R. (2009) *Long-term Personal Data Storage*, www.zdnet.com/blog/storage/long-term-personal-data-storage/376.

Heery, R. and Powell, A. (2006) *Digital Repositaries Roadmap: looking forward*, UKOLN and Eduserv Foundation.

Helmore, E. (2010) Tina Brown's Daily Beast bids for Newsweek – and a showdown with the Huffington Post, *Guardian*, www.guardian.co.uk/media/2010/oct/07/tina-brown-daily-beast-newsweek.

Hemp, P. (2009) Death by Information Overload, *Harvard Business Review*, **87** (9), 82–9.

Henry, N. (1974) Knowledge Management: a new concern for public administration, *Public Administration Review*, **34** (3), 189–96.

Herrman, J. and Buchanan, M. (2010) *The Future of Storage*,
  http://gizmodo.com/5497512/the-future-of-storage.

Hill, K. (2011) Yes, the CIA's 'Ninja Librarians' Are Tracking Twitter and Facebook
  (As They Should), *Forbes*, www.forbes.com/sites/kashmirhill/2011/11/09/
  yes-the-cias-ninja-librarians-are-tracking-twitter-and-facebook-as-they-should.

Hitchcock, G. (2011) British Museum Makes the Wikipedia Connection, *Guardian*,
  www.guardian.co.uk/government-computing-network/2011/aug/08/
  british-museum-wikipedia.

Hyams, E. (2011a) Making Sense of the World with Ranganathan and a Fluffy Toy,
  CILIP Update, September, 21–3.

Hyams, E. (2011b) What's New in the E-content Market?, *CILIP Update*, November
  2011, 37–40.

Internet Archive (2011) *About the Internet Archive*,
  www.archive.org/about/about.php.

Isenberg, D. (1998) The Dawn of the Stupid Network, *ACM netWorker*, **2** (1), 24–31.

Jackson, J. (2010) *Google: 129 million different books have been published*,
  www.pcworld.com/article/202803/google_129_million_different_books_
  have_been_published.html.

Jackson, S. (2011) Retail Softness Hits Newspaper Sales, *The Australian*,
  www.theaustralian.com.au/media/retail-softness-hits-newspaper-sales/
  story-e6frg996-1226054950712.

Jarvis, J. (2009) *What Would Google Do?*, Collins.

Kalish, J. (2010) Talking Tech and Building an Empire from Podcasts, *New York Times*,
  www.nytimes.com/2010/12/27/technology/27podcast.html?_r-3&ref-technology#.

Kidd, A. (2003) *Document Retention: the IT manager's changing role*,
  www.techrepublic.com/article/document-retention-the-it-managers-changing-
  role/5054924.

Knopper, S. (2009) *Appetite for Self-destruction: the spectacular crash of the record
  industry in the digital age*, Free Press.

Lau, A. (2011) *Yahoo's Shashi Seth on the Future of Search, Mobile & Structured Data*,
  http://searchenginewatch.com/article/2114498/Yahoos-Shashi-Seth-on-the-Future-
  of-Search-Mobile-Structured-Data.

Lee, M. and Lan, Y. (2007) From Web 2.0 to Conversational Knowledge: towards
  collaborative intelligence, *Journal of Entrepreneurship Research*, **2** (2), 47–62.

Lehrer, J. (2010) Our Cluttered Minds, *New York Times*,
  www.nytimes.com/2010/06/06/books/review/Lehrer-t.html.

Leiner, B. et al. (2009) A Brief History of the Internet, *ACM SIGCOMM Computer
  Communication Review*, **38** (5), 22–31.

Lesk, M. (1997) *How Much Information Is There In the World?*
  www.lesk.com/mlesk/ksg97/ksg.html.

Lessig, L. (2011) *Adobe in Wonderland*,
   www.lessig.org/content/standard/0,1902,22914,00.html.
Levie, A. (2011) *The Smarter Enterprise*,
   http://gigaom.com/collaboration/the-smarter-enterprise.
Levy, M. (2009) Web 2.0 Implications on Knowledge Management, *Journal of Knowledge Management*, **13** (1), 120–34.
Libbenga, J. (2011) *Sweden Postpones EU Data Retention Directive, Faces Court, Fines*,
   www.theregister.co.uk/2011/03/18/sweden_postpones_eu_data_retention_directive/.
Luckhurst, T. (2011) Black and White and Dead All Over?, *Times Higher Education*, (8 September), 38.
Lyman, P. and Varian, H. R. (2000) How Much Information?, *Journal of Electronic Publishing*, **6** (2).
Lyman, P. and Varian, H. R. (2003) *How Much Information?*,
   www2.sims.berkeley.edu/research/projects/how-much-info-2003.
Lynch, C. (2003) Institutional Repositories: essential infrastructure for scholarship in the digital age, *ARL Bimonthly Report*, 226.
Machlup, F. (1962) *The Production and Distribution of Knowledge in the United States*, Princeton University Press.
Manyika, J. and Roxburgh, C. (2011) *The Great Transformer: the impact of the internet on economic growth and prosperity*, McKinsey Global Institute,
   www.mckinsey.com/Insights/MGI/Research/Technology_and_Innovation/The_great_transformer.
Manyika, J. et al. (2011) *Big Data: the next frontier for innovation, competition, and productivity*, McKinsey Global Institute,
   www.mckinsey.com/Insights/MGI/Research/Technology_and_Innovation/Big_data_The_next_frontier_for_innovation.
Maxcer, C. (2007) *Fail-Safe System Fails in Alaska's Data Debacle*,
   www.technewsworld.com/rsstory/56414.html.
McAfee, A. (2009) *Enterprise 2.0: new collaborative tools for your organization's toughest challenges*, Harvard Business School Press.
McCandless, D. (2010) *How Much Do Music Artists Earn Online?*,
   www.informationisbeautiful.net/2010/how-much-do-music-artists-earn-online.
McGee, M. (2010) By the Numbers: Twitter vs. Facebook vs. Google Buzz, Search Engine Land, http://searchengineland.com/by-the-numbers-twitter-vs-facebook-vs-google-buzz-36709.
Merced, M. (2011) Who Will Profit from AOL's Deal for Huffington Post?, *New York Times*, http://dealbook.nytimes.com/2011/02/07/who-will-cash-out-of-aols-huffpo-deal.
Miller, C. and Bilton, N. (2011) Google's Lab of Wildest Dreams, *New York Times*,

www.nytimes.com/2011/11/14/technology/at-google-x-a-top-secret-lab-dreaming-up-the-future.html.

Miller, R. (2010) *Iron Mountain's Energy Efficient Bunker,* www.datacenterknowledge.com/iron-mountains-energy-efficient-bunker.

Miller, R. (2011) *Report: Google uses about 900,000 servers,* www.datacenterknowledge.com/archives/2011/08/01/report-google-uses-about-900000-servers.

Mitchell, A., Christian, L. and Rosenstiel, T. (2011) *The Tablet Revolution and What It Means for the Future of News,* Pew Research Center, http://pewresearch.org/pubs/2119/tablet-news.

National Archives (2011) *The United Kingdom Report on the Re-use of Public Sector Information,* www.nationalarchives.gov.uk/documents/information-management/psi-report.pdf.

Newton, M., Miller, C. and Stowell Bracke, M. (2011) Librarian Roles in Institutional Repository Data Set Collecting: outcomes of a research library task force, *Collection Management,* **36** (1), 53–67.

Nonaka, I. and Takeuchi, H. (1995) *The Knowledge Creating Company: how Japanese companies create the dynasties of innovation,* Oxford University Press.

OECD (2010) *The Evolution of News and the Internet,* Organisation for Economic Co-operation and Development, www.oecd.org/dataoecd/30/24/45559596.pdf.

OECD (2011) *OECD Broadband Portal,* Organisation for Economic Co-operation and Development, www.oecd.org/sti/ict/broadband.

Ofcom (2011) *Communications Market Report,* Ofcom.

ONS (2011) *Internet Access – households and individuals,* 2011, Office for National Statistics, www.ons.gov.uk/ons/rel/rdit2/internet-access-households-and-individuals/ 2011/stb-internet-access-2011.html.

Pang, B. and Lee, L. (2008) Opinion Mining and Sentiment Analysis, *Foundations and Trends in Information Retrieval,* **2** (1–2), 1–135.

Pariser, E. (2011) *The Filter Bubble: what the internet is hiding from you,* Viking.

Pauly, D. (2009) *EU Data Retention Directive – golden rules for ISPs,* www.telecoms.com/17337/eu-data-retention-directive-%E2%80%93-golden-rules-for-isps/.

Phillips, H. (2010) The Great Library of Alexandria?, *Library Philosophy and Practice,* August.

PIRA (2000) *Commercial Exploitation of Europe's Public Sector Information,* PIRA International.

Radicati Group (2010) *Key Statistics for Email, Instant Messaging, Social Networking and Wireless Email,* www.radicati.com/?p=5290.

Rao, L. (2011) *Apple's App Store Crosses 15B App Downloads, Adds 1B Downloads in Past Month,* http://techcrunch.com/2011/07/07/apples-app-store-crosses-15b-app-downloads-adds-1b-downloads-in-past-month.

Rethlefsen, M. (2010) Checking In: location services for libraries, *Library Journal,* www.libraryjournal.com/article/CA6725234.html.

Rosenbloom, S. (2007) On Facebook, Scholars Link Up With Data, *New York Times*, www.nytimes.com/2007/12/17/style/17facebook.html?_r=2&sq=d.

Sabbagh, D. (2011) Times Paywall Tops 100,000 – but can it grow much further at that price?, *Guardian*, www.guardian.co.uk/media/organgrinder/2011/jul/03/times-paywall-revenue.

Sandvine (2011) *Sandvine's Spring 2011 Global Internet Phenomena Report Reveals New Internet Trends*, www.sandvine.com/news/pr_detail.asp?ID=312.

Schumpeter, J. (1950) *Capitalism, Socialism, and Democracy*, 3rd edn, Harper.

Schwartz, B. (2010) *Yahoo UK & Ireland Directory Closing November 8, 2010*, http://searchengineland.com/yahoo-uk-ireland-directory-closing-november-8-2010-52405.

SCONUL (1999) *Information Skills in Higher Education: a SCONUL position paper*, www.sconul.ac.uk/groups/information_literacy/seven_pillars.html.

SearchEngineWatch (2011) *New YouTube Statistics: 48 hours of video uploaded per minute; 3 billion views per day*, http://searchenginewatch.com/article/2073962/New-YouTube-Statistics-48-Hours-of-Video-Uploaded-Per-Minute-3-Billion-Views-Per-Day

Shapiro, C. and Varian, H. (1999) *Information Rules*, Harvard Business School Press.

Smith, I. (2010) *Cost of Hard Drive Storage Space*, http://ns1758.ca/winch/winchest.html.

Stevenson, V. and Hodges, S. (2008) Setting Up a University Digital Repository: experience with DigiTool, *OCLC Systems and Services: International Digital Library Perspectives*, **24** (1), 48–50.

Stonier, T. (1983) *The Wealth of Information*, Thames Methuen.

Toffler, A. (1970) *Future Shock*, The Bodley Head.

Toffler, A. (1980) *The Third Wave*, Bantam Books.

Toffler, A. (1990) *Powershift: knowledge, wealth and violence at the edge of the 21st century*, Bantam Books.

University of Virginia Library (2011) *AIMS – born digital collections: an inter-institutional model for stewardship*, www2.lib.virginia.edu/aims.

Vasquez, R. and Shiffler, G. (2011) *Forecast: PC installed base, worldwide, 2006–2015, March 2011 update*, www.gartner.com/DisplayDocument?id=1602818.

Wachter, S. (2010) Beaming to the Cloud All the Mess That Is Our Digital Life, *New York Times*, www.nytimes.com/2010/10/25/technology/25iht-clutter25.html.

Wang, M. (2007) Introducing CRM Into an Academic Library, *Library Management*, **28** (6/7), 281–91.

Watson Hall (2011) *UK Data Retention Requirements*, https://www.watsonhall.com/resources/downloads/paper-uk-data-retention-requirements.pdf.

Waxman, L. et al. (2007) The Library as Place: providing students with opportunities for socialization, relaxation, and restoration, *New Library World*, **108** (9/10), 424–34.

Weber, L. (2009) *Marketing to the Social Web: how digital customer communities build your business*, John Wiley & Sons.

Williams, C. (2011) How Egypt Shut Down the Internet, *Telegraph*, www.telegraph.co.uk/news/worldnews/africaandindianocean/egypt/8288163/How-Egypt-shut-down-the-internet.html.

Williams, J. (2011) Worldwide Smartphone Sales Grow 74% in Second Quarter of 2011, says Gartner, *Computer Weekly*, www.computerweekly.com/news/2240105329/Worldwide-smartphone-sales-grow-74-in-second-quarter-of-2011-says-Gartner.

Williams, M. (2005) *Gale Directory of Databases*, Gale Group.

Wilson, T. (2002) The Nonsense of Knowledge Management, *Information Research*, **8** (1).

Woodward, H. and Estelle, L. (2010) *Digital Information: order or anarchy?* Facet Publishing.

Yarrow, J. (2011) *Amazon Will Get 10% of its Revenue from Kindle in 2012*, http://articles.businessinsider.com/2011-06-07/tech/29961480_1_amazon-s-kindle-kindle-business-mark-mahaney.

Zittrain, J. (2008) *The Future of the Internet*, Yale University Press.

Index

academic publishing
    see also education delivery
    institutional repositories (IRs)
        41–4
academies
    information storage 41–4
    research storage 41–4
advertising, targeted
    Facebook 27 9
    Google 25–7
    information production 25–9
Al-Nakaash, Paul, information
        providers 8–10
Allen, David, Getting Things Done
        (GTD) 107
Alterian SM2, information
        monitoring 34–5
amateur vs professional
        blogs/blogging 18
Amazon
    digital rights management
        (DRM) 95–8
    e-books 93–8
    information consumption 93–4
    Kindle 93–8
answer-engines, future search 113–14

apps
    HTML5 99–101
    smartphones 92–3

B2B publishing *see* business
        publishing
'big data'
    challenges 6–8, 31–5
    data analytics/management 31–5
    data types 33–5
    monitoring 34–5
    supermarkets 32–4
    Tesco 32, 34
    Walmart 34
Bing, answer-engine 113–14
Bintliff, E., business publishing 21
bittorrent technology, file sharing
        67–8
blogs/blogging
    amateur vs professional 18
    business publishing 19–22
    challenge to publishers 14–22
    GigaOm 22
    Huffington Post 17–19
    information production 14–22
    Luckhurst, T. 18

blogs/blogging (*continued*)
  vs newspapers 15–18
  vs print media 15–22
Born Digital project, digitizing
  collections 50
Brindley, Lynne, digitizing
  collections 49
British Library, digitizing collections
  49
British Museum, Wikipedia
  collaboration 25
Burley, D., HTML5 100
business intelligence, business
  publishing 21
business publishing
  Bintliff, E. 21
  blogs/blogging 19–22
  business intelligence 21
  Fenez, M. 20
  GigaOm 22
  van Der Donk, M. 20

Cane, A., information as strategic
  capital asset 32
Carr, N., internet 103
Central Office of Information (COI),
  government, public
  engagement with 76
cloud information storage 53–4, 55
cold climate information storage 41,
  57–8
collaborative publishing
  information production 22–5
  wikis 22–5
collection digitization *see* digitizing
  collections
company reputations, analysing
  114–16
content farms
  Google 118–19
  search engines 118–19

copyright
  Creative Commons 117–18
  digital rights management
    (DRM) 95–8, 117
  implications for publishers 117–18
copyright-friendly intermediaries
  internet 68–9
  iTunes 68–9
corporate data
  information storage 44–5
  legal requirements 44–5
costs, information storage 57
creating information, new ways 10
Creative Commons, implications for
  publishers 117–18

data
  see also information
  'big data' 6–8, 31–5
  information 2–3
  Manyika *et al.* 8
  terminology 2–3
  types 33–5
data analytics/management
  'big data' 31–5
  information monitoring 34–5
  traditional library and
    information courses 33
Data Liberation Front, Google 54–5
data mining 46–8
  see also data
    analytics/management
  customer relationship
    management (CRM) 46–8
  Tesco 46–8
  Walmart 46–8
'database of intentions', Google 25–7
database provision, internet impact
  64–5, 86–7
devices, information consumption
  67–9, 86–93, 118–19

digital footprints 54–6
  Facebook 54–6
digital information, 'first-copy costs'
  66
digital rights management (DRM)
  e-books 95–8
  implications for publishers 117
digitizing collections
  Born Digital project 50
  British Library 49
  Domesday Project 50
  information storage 48–51
directory of websites, Yahoo! 39
disintermediation
  information distribution 63–6
  internet 63–6
DNA, information storage 58
Domesday Project, digitizing
    collections 50
DRM *see* digital rights management

e-books 93–8
  digital rights management
    (DRM) 95–8
  lending 97–8
  resale 96–7
e-prints
  institutional repositories (IRs)
    43–4
  University of Southampton 43–4
education delivery
  see also academic publishing
  internet 71–2
  Khan Academy 72
Encyclopaedia Britannica 24
ePetitions, public engagement with
    government 77
European Union Data Retention
    Directive (EUDRD)
  information storage 45–6
  legal requirements 45–6

Facebook
  digital footprints 54–6
  information production 27–9
  information storage 54–6
  targeted advertising 27–9
Fenez, M., business publishing 20
financial markets, internet impact
    65–6
'first-copy costs', digital information
    66
future
  information storage 56–8
  search 113–14

generative internet 80–2
Getting Things Done (GTD)
  Allen, David 107
  information overload 107
Gibson, A., public engagement with
    government 76
GigaOm
  blogs/blogging 22
  business publishing 22
Google
  content farms 118–19
  Data Liberation Front 54–5
  'database of intentions' 25–7
  information literacy 103–6
  information production 25–7
  information storage 41, 54–5
  Panda search algorithm 118–19
  search algorithm 118–19
  smart devices 121
  targeted advertising 25–7
Google Scholar 43
government
  Central Office of Information
    (COI) 76
  defensive 74–5
  ePetitions 77
  Open Data Institute 79

government (*continued*)
    open government 73–9
    proactive 73–4
    public engagement 75–7
    public sector information (PSI)
        77–9
Great Library of Alexandria,
    information storage 38–9
GTD *see* Getting Things Done

Halliday, J., internet preferential
    services 80–2
Heery, R., institutional repositories
    (IRs) 42
historical background, information
    storage 37–9
HTML5
    apps 99–101
    open web 99–101
Huffington Post, blogs/blogging
    17–19
Hyams, E.
    data analytics/management 33
    traditional library and
        information courses 33

implications for information
    professionals 111–16
    see also opportunities/threats
    information consumption 107–9
    knowledge management
        opportunity 112–13
    libraries 107–9
    search, future 113–14
implications for publishers 116–20
    content farms 118–19
    copyright challenge 117–18
    Creative Commons 117–18
    digital rights management
        (DRM) 117
    tablet computers 119–20

implications for society 120–2
    'internet everywhere' 121–2
    personal privacy 121–2
    smart devices 121
information
    see also data
    creating, new ways of 10
    data 2–3
    global amount 1
    importance 11–12
    monitoring 34–5
    terminology 2–3
information consumption 85–109
    Amazon 93–4
    database provision 64–5, 86–7
    devices 67–9, 86–93
    implications for information
        professionals 107–9
    information literacy 103–6
    information overload 106–7
    iPods 90–1
    location-based services 108–9
    mobile devices 88–93, 118–19
    music-playing devices 67–9,
        90–1
    operating systems 91–3
    Pariser, E. 105–6
    smartphones 90–3
information distribution 59–83
    disintermediation 63–6
    intermediaries 66–9
    internet architecture 60–3
    online video 69–73
    open government 73–9
    opportunities/threats 80–2
information literacy 103–6
    defining 104
    Google 103–6
    information consumption
        103–6
    internet impact 103–4

Society of College, National and
University Libraries (SCONUL)
105
information monitoring 34–5
see also data analytics/
management; data mining
information overload 106–7
Getting Things Done (GTD) 107
information processing, Search,
Links, Authorship, Tags,
Extensions, Signalling
(SLATES) 116
information production 13–35
blogs/blogging 14–22
business publishing 19–22
challenges 31–5
collaborative publishing 22–5
Facebook 27–9
Google 25–7
podcasting 29–31
print media economics 15–18
search engines 25–9
social networks 27–9
strategic capital asset 31–5
targeted advertising 25–9
wikis 22–5
information providers, challenges
8–10
information society, foundations 3–4
information storage 10–11, 37–58
academies 41–4
cloud 53–4, 55
cold climate 41, 57–8
corporate data 44–5
costs 38, 41, 57
data mining 46–8
digital footprints 54–6
digitizing collections 48–51
directory of websites 39
DNA 58
European Union Data Retention
Directive (EUDRD) 45–6
Facebook 54–6
future 56–8
Google 41, 54–5
Great Library of Alexandria 38–9
historical background 37–9
institutional repositories (IRs)
41–4
Internet Archive 39–40
internet, preserving 38–41
internet service providers (ISPs)
45–6
legal requirements 44–6
mountain storage 51
offsite 51, 53–4
Patriot Act 2001: 45
personal level 51–3
private sector 44
research storage 41–4
Sarbanes-Oxley Act (SOX) 44–5
security 51, 53–4
solid state drives (SSDs) 57
Yahoo! 39
institutional repositories (IRs)
academic publishing 41–4
e-prints 43–4
information storage 41–4
Open Archives Initiative Protocol
for Metedata Harvesting
(OAIOMH) 43
University of Southampton 43–4
interactive television 61–2
intermediaries
disintermediation, information
distribution 63–6
information distribution 66–9
internet
architecture 60–3
background 3–4
bittorrent technology 67–8
Carr, N. 103

internet (*continued*)
  copyright-friendly intermediaries
    68–9
  database provision, impact on
    64–5, 86–7
  devices, information
    consumption 67–9, 86–93,
    118–19
  disintermediation 63–6
  distribution 63–9
  driver of change 4–6
  education delivery 71–2
  evolution 3–4
  financial markets 65–6
  generative 80–2
  historic development 60–3
  information literacy 103–4
  information storage 38–41
  infrastructure 60–3
  interactive television 61–2
  'internet everywhere' 121–2
  iTunes 68–9
  Khan Academy 72
  Leiner, B. 60
  Massachusetts Institute of
    Technology (MIT) 60
  media industry 67–73, 101–2
  mobile devices, information
    consumption 88–93
  music industry 67–73, 101–2
  network neutrality 81–2
  open government 73–9
  opportunities/threats 4–6
  origins 60
  preferential services 80–2
  preserving 38–41
  publishing industry changes
    4–6
  smart devices 121
  StockTwits 65–6
  telephony services 81
  transient nature of web pages
    38–41
  video 69–73
  world wide web (WWW) 62
  YouTube 69–73
Internet Archive, information
  storage 39–40
'internet everywhere', implications
  for society 121–2
internet service providers (ISPs)
  information storage 45–6
  legal requirements 45–6
iPods 90
IRs *see* institutional repositories
ISPs *see* internet service providers
iTunes, copyright-friendly
  intermediary 68–9

Jarvis, J.
  newspapers 16
  Universities, value-adding 71–2

Khan Academy, education delivery
  72
Kindle, e-books 93–8
knowledge management
  opportunity 112–13

legal requirements
  corporate data 44–5
  European Union Data Retention
    Directive (EUDRD) 45–6
  information storage 44–6
  internet service providers (ISPs)
    45–6
  Patriot Act 2001: 45
  Sarbanes-Oxley Act (SOX)
    44–5
Leiner, B., internet 60
libraries
  configurations 107–9

libraries (*continued*)
  implications for information
    professionals 107–9
  opportunities/threats 5–6
location-based services 108–9
Luckhurst, T., blogs/blogging 18

Manyika *et al.*, data importance 8
Massachusetts Institute of
    Technology (MIT), internet 60
media industry
  bittorrent technology 67–8
  internet impact 67–73, 101–2
MIT *see* Massachusetts Institute of
    Technology
mobile devices
  information consumption 88–93,
    118–19
  tablet computers 118–19
monitoring information 34–5
  see also data analytics/
    management; data mining
mountain storage, security 51
music industry, internet impact
    67–73, 101–2
music-playing devices 67–9, 90–1

Napster, file sharing 67
network neutrality
  internet 81–2
  open web 81–2
newspapers
  vs blogs/blogging 15–18
  costs of producing 15–16
  economics 15–18
  Jarvis, J. 16
ninja librarians 114–16

offsite information storage 51, 53–4
Open Archives Initiative Protocol
    for Metedata Harvesting

(OAIOMH), institutional
    repositories (IRs) 43
Open Data Institute
  government 79
  public sector information (PSI)
    79
open government 73–9
open web 98–101
  HTML5 99–101
  network neutrality 81–2
  opportunities/threats 80–2
  preferential services 80–2
  telephony services 81
  Zittrain, J. 80–1
operating systems, information
    consumption 91–3
opportunities/threats
  see also implications for
    information professionals
  information distribution 80–2
  internet 4–6
  knowledge management
    opportunity 112–13
  libraries 5 6
  open web 80–2

Panda search algorithm, Google
    118–19
Pariser, E., information
    consumption 105–6
Patriot Act 2001:
  information storage 45
  legal requirements 45
personal level information storage
    51–3
personal privacy, implications for
    society 121–2
The Pirate Bay, file sharing 67–8
podcasting
  information production 29–31
  TWiT network 30–1

Powell, A., institutional repositories (IRs) 42
print media
    vs blogs/blogging 15–22
    business publishing 19–22
    economics 15–18
    newspapers 15–18
private sector, information storage 44
professional vs amateur blogs/blogging 18
PSI *see* public sector information
public engagement, government 75–7
public sector information (PSI)
    European Directive 78–9
    government 77–9
    making money from 77–9
    Open Data Institute 79
    repackaging/reusing 77–9
publishing industry changes, internet 4–6

Radian6, information monitoring 34–5
repackaging/reusing public sector information (PSI) 77–9

Sarbanes-Oxley Act (SOX)
    information storage 44–5
    legal requirements 44–5
SCONUL *see* Society of College, National and University Libraries
search algorithm, Google 118–19
search engines
    answer-engines 113–14
    Bing 113–14
    content farms 118–19
    Google, 'database of intentions' 25–7

Google, search algorithm 118–19
    information production 25–9
    Panda search algorithm 118–19
search, future 113–14
    answer-engines 113–14
    Siri voice recognition 114
    Wolfram Alpha 114
Search, Links, Authorship, Tags, Extensions, Signalling (SLATES), information processing 116
security
    cloud information storage 53–4, 55
    information storage 51, 53–4
    mountain storage 51
    offsite information storage 51, 53–4
Shapiro, C.
    'first-copy costs' 66
    publishing industry changes 6
Siri voice recognition, future search 114
SLATES *see* Search, Links, Authorship, Tags, Extensions, Signalling
smart devices, internet 121
smartphones, information consumption 90–3
social networks
    company reputations, analysing 114–16
    Facebook 27–9
    information production 27–9
Society of College, National and University Libraries (SCONUL), information literacy 105
solid state drives (SSDs), information storage 57

StockTwits
   internet 65–6
   Twitter 65–6
storing information *see* information
      storage
strategic capital asset, information
      production 31–5
supermarkets, 'big data' 32–4

tablet computers, implications for
      publishers 119–20
targeted advertising, information
      production 25–9
telephony services
   open web 81
   smartphones 90–2
terminology
   data 2–3
   information 2–3
Tesco
   'big data' 32, 34
   data mining 46–8
threats *see* opportunities/threats
traditional library and information
      courses, data analytics/
      management 33
TWiT network, podcasting 30–1
Twitter, StockTwits 65–6

Universities, value-adding 71–2
University of Southampton
   e-prints 43–4

institutional repositories (IRs)
      43–4

van Der Donk, M., business
      publishing 20
Varian, H.
   'first-copy costs' 66
   publishing industry changes 6
video
   internet 69–73
   YouTube 69–73

Walmart
   'big data' 34
   data mining 46–8
WikiLeaks 75
Wikipedia 23–5
wikis
   collaborative publishing 22–5
   information production 22–5
Wolfram Alpha, answer-engine 114
world wide web (WWW),
      development 62

Yahoo!
   directory of websites 39
   information storage 39
YouTube 69–73

Zittrain, J.
   generative internet 80–1
   open web 80–1